ST. MARY'S ... ... RY
ST. ... W9-DHN-357 ... ...LAND)

UTOPIA 1976

31458

UTOPIA 1976

by *Morris L. Ernst*

Leopold

GREENWOOD PRESS, PUBLISHERS
NEW YORK

Copyright © 1955 by Joan E. Goldstein

Reprinted by permission
of Greenbaum, Wolff & Ernst

First Greenwood Reprinting 1969

Library of Congress Catalogue Card Number 73-90502

SBN 8371-2325-9

PRINTED IN UNITED STATES OF AMERICA

To Nicholas, Debbie and Steffie,
who will be able to prove whether
the old man was right or wrong.
And to Marie Jahoda, who does
not have to wait until 1976.

CONTENTS

UTOPIA 1976

Chapter 1

WHY I WRITE A UTOPIA

THIS BOOK IS MY UTOPIA. IT IS A DREAM FOR OUR REPUBLIC in 1976. It is a dream within reach—a dream capable of attainment if only more of us hold dreams of similar hope. I tell about our vast new leisure arising from new sources of energy and the chemical revolution on our farms. I will not avoid my fears of statism through industrial concentrations.

But beyond these Facts of 1976 I know that all of the glamour of less work and more income has little reality except as the home, the family, the school—as well as the mental and physical health of our people—are enriched in spiritual terms. Above all—we can only lead rich full lives if our society is conducted with freedom and order—by the processes of religion, government, law and an honorable search for truth and peace.

I am sure of my Utopia. My dream is based for the

most part on nothing more than an extension of present trends. If I appear overoptimistic, I rest my defense on my studies of many Utopias written by other optimists over the ages.

Man has much in common with all other species on our planet—the need for food for his body, energy for his brain, and shelter against unfriendly weather. Although not to be completely analogized, man's sexual, or even his distinguishable parental, urge is not entirely unlike that of some other animals. We possess, however, one unique asset capable either of inaction or adventure—a brain more highly developed than that of any other animal. This provides us with the rare enrichment of a history— that is, a knowledge of change in social organizations. On the other hand, a society of termites of 2000 B.C. in China is identic with current termite societies. But oddly enough, we are less aware of our own vestigial patterns than we are of the circular downbedding of a dog who treats a parlor rug as his ancestors used the soft leaves in the forest.

One of the clearest differences between us and other animals may well arise from an ineffable talent for contemplation. I doubt if a cow's inaction is equivalent to an act of reverie. So far as we know, neither the lion nor the lamb contemplates the miracles of birth or the amazements of death. Possibly our distinguishing trait is that no other animal expects, or dreams about, a tomorrow. At no time has man failed to scribble the projections of his future on earth and, as if man could not endure the concept of the limitations of his earthly existence, he groped for oracles and prophets of his future nonmortal life. The Elysian fields of the Greeks were the Happy Hunting Grounds of the Indians, and for those who would not embrace a joyous fantasy of the future, Nirvana—a forgetfulness—was the answer that offered relief. Over the entire brief period of recorded history—say five thousand years—leadership was wedded to *Nowheres* of the future, while prophets interpreted in changing fashions the rewards or punishments of the hereafter. In our own culture these were called Heaven or Hell, moderated by a God created in man's own image. It is not irreligious to suggest that if lions have a god it probably looks and acts pretty much like a lion.

I have read Utopias from Plato of Greece in the fourth century B.C., to Bellamy of the United States in 1887. Writings of these entrancing speculators endured through the centuries because the authors were men of hope. That they were not precisely delphic is irrelevant, for what does it matter that it took nearly five hundred years before Sir Thomas More's prophecy of a six-hour work day should come into being? The interesting fact is that any man in a culture where the battle for existence required a sixteen-hour work day seven days a week should have possessed a mind with a leap sufficient to think of a six-hour, five-day work week. This capacity of man to get outside of his own frame of reference—a kind of intellectual Icarian hope—must be viewed against the position of Judge Gary, the astute head of one of our vast steel companies, who around

1910 predicted that some steel-mill workers must *always* work a twelve-hour day if steel is to be produced in our nation.

Surely it is not fortuitous that former Utopias have stayed in print for so long as a part of man's preferred literary diet. Plato, more than two thousand years ago, set forth his ideas of a perfect future culture, and of the ingredients of an ultimate form of government. His writings still have a modernity in relation to this century. Sir Thomas More's *Utopia* (published in Latin in 1516) can be bought in English in inexpensive reprint form after more than four hundred years. About a century thereafter Francis Bacon, in his *New Atlantis,* used science as the springboard for his dream of man's forward march. Fourrier in France toyed with a society wherein boys of ten to twelve years of age would clean the sewers and enjoy it—a form of universal civilian training. Robert Owen vitalized the future of the cooperative, and Samuel Butler's *Erewhon* (1872) supplied an easy reversal of title for *News from Nowhere,* wherein the gracious William Morris used a fiction form to spread his own tender predictions of the full life which man could attain. Edward Bellamy, an American newspaperman, in *Looking Backward* burned a human corpse in Boston in 1887 and resurrected him in the same city 113 years later, in the year 2000. This book sold hundreds of thousands of copies and was responsible for a spate of more than three hundred novels speculating on man's hopeful future—*on earth.*

All the Utopias which have persisted in man's reading favor have been based on optimism, even though none would meet in its detailed prognosis our present tests of reality or even the magnitude of our future hopes. The writings of glandular pessimists, of men too scared to hope, evaporate into limbo as soon as the type has been unscrambled. One of the most recent tomes of despair, *1984* by George Orwell, catered to all those who enjoyed the masochism of seeing man at a crossroad with all direction markers pointing to chaos. Such pessimism appears even in the pleasant writings of our longest distance viewer, Charles Galton Darwin, who penned in 1953 *The Next Million Years* as his manifesto of the ultimate though less than proximate end of man. I suggest that Darwin enjoys his present life while he predicts the final destruction of the human race. Artists often depict doom as a catharsis for the guilts of their own gaiety.

During our lifetime one Utopia has, whether we like it or not, deeply affected in dire terms the entire history of our epoch. Under a candle or oil lamp, in 1847, Karl Heinrich Marx and Friedrich Engels wrote *Das Kommunistiche Manifest*. This brief pamphlet preached hope for the oppressed, hope based on hatred and bitterness, hope derived from malice for many, and charity for none—but nevertheless *hope*. The compassion its authors expressed in light of the economics of their Europe was not only passionately resisted by some but passionately accepted by others. Most of the pamphlet is totally irrelevant today, and even in 1847 the major part was little more than a tidbit of contemporary journalism. But the core of this document promptly scared the leaders of wealth and government throughout Europe and gathered momentum, in part, because of the sporadic and repeated attempts to suppress it. This bitter gospel of cheer for the downtrodden proffered hope on earth at a time when man's only hope was said to exist after his death. Naturally it was resisted more than all previous Utopias had been by the leaders of the churches. Other Utopias were not so clearly antithetical to the heaven concept of most religions. Increasingly it created a feeling of guilt among the many men and women of wealth who felt uncomfortable living in the midst of people gnawed by hunger. The fact that the hope of this manifesto sprang from hatred seemed only to accent the dream, for it created ambivalent emotions: hope for man on the one hand and an opportunity to drain off pent-up envies on the other. Psychological resistances to fathers and mothers unconsciously swelled the ranks of communist adherents.

The economic base from which Marx and Engels derived their class hates and workers' dreams has been proven invalid. The underlying facts were scarcely scrutinized by those who, following selfless men and later women, were susceptible to promises of pie on earth instead of pie in the sky, without regard to any tight logic or factual proof.

This was the most effective piece of literature of the last century and it helped propel many people in our land—non-Marxists—because of personal bewilderments,

to cry out with despair: "We are facing chaos," or
"The atomic bomb spells the end of our civilization."
Such slogans of desperation are often sequelled by exhor-
tations of "Follow ME." But typical of the people of our
Republic very few follow, for we do not casually line up
behind leaders who stand at a crossroad not knowing
which path to choose. People follow only the optimists
and never the negators of life.

It should be noted that aside from Marx (who de-
rided Utopias, claiming to have a scientific formula) none
of the authors of enduring Utopias pegged his prophecies
on economic data or extrapolation of known facts. Even
Jefferson, a hopeful who liked the dreams of the future
even more than the history of the past, wrote less in terms
statistical than did Alexander Hamilton, a far more limited and often despairing Utopian. Lord Bryce, at the
time of Bellamy, in his *American Commonwealth* (1888)
—optimist that he was—saw that both the American
workman and millionaire had a "larger head of steam on
than his father had." But such analysis was not objectively
documented, and the trends which he discussed were unrelated to any statistical proof of our expanding economy.

When postulating a Utopia it is obviously simpler to
pick a date in the far distant future, than one near by.
Imagination can soar with less restraint of potential cor-
rection if one dreams of a date beyond the life expectancy
of one's audience. No doubt such considerations have led
those who speculated on man's future to adopt a mood
not remote from the literature of escape. If a writer pitches

his aim at a target far, far off, he can assume without fear of contradiction that all has changed, even that prime force called human nature.

I have followed with amusement the talmudic debates about the relative impacts of heredity and environment, and I sit on the sidelines favoring, maybe only out of wishful thinking, the biologists who argue that the susceptibility of dogs to learning tricks is an inheritable trait. And although I am inclined to believe that a good Latin scholar possesses no identifiable "Latin genes" to pass on to his heir, nevertheless, as James Harvey Robinson said: "We can invent more and more mind" now that we have learned the trick. I need no confirmation of my own faith in the overwhelming biological adaptability of man to learn vast additional tricks in the backward and youthful art of living.

My discountable prejudices are far more obvious, I am sure, and far more readily admitted, I hope. I have reread the famous Utopias with peculiar interest because I am at the tail end of my life, and while I find the memory of my early youth increases its backward reaches, my dreams and hopes seem to stretch always further into the future. Maybe this will help to explain why Utopias are seldom the product of youth, and why the age of the author is not entirely irrelevant for proper appraisal of his writings. Soon, I hope, some woman will pioneer in the Utopian fields.

Another discountable factor is that Life has consistently cast her more favored dice in my direction. I have been lucky beyond the point where I need pinch myself any more. Above all, I have, as far back as my memory goes, carried on a love affair, an enduring romance, with the Republic of the United States. As an incurable glandular optimist my hopes at times have been bruised, but with the bounce of an optimist, I confess that I still see the glass of wine half full, and never half empty. Increasingly I find that the press, radio and movies—the pipe lines to the minds of our people—predominately report the dregs of the glass, the sordid and the painful, emphasizing fear and cynicism rather than what to me are clear signs of the first great mass renaissance of man on this planet.

This Utopia I shall write was first aimed to hit the target year—2000. That millennial figure is an attractive round number, containing three of those gay integers, those good round o's. But soon, as a check on my own expansiveness, I found I would less likely depart from truth if I shot at an earlier date. So I took the year 1976. It had the obvious flavor of being two hundred years after we declared ourselves a nation. Moreover, the great majority of readers of today will live until 1976, while only a small minority will beat the mortality table at the year 2000.

I would be less than frank if I did not admit a few of my most obvious limitations. Above all, I believe in acts of faith, the most precious of which is my belief that truth wins out in the open market place of thought, or at least has a better chance of so doing than any other method known to man. I must confess I know of no empirical proof of this truly religious act, which is the matrix of our culture—the ever expanding concept imbedded in the First Amendment of our Constitution.

Then again, I hold those to be right who believe with me that the purpose of life is not merely to fill bellies and build roofs. Nor is the full life of man to be built by amassing tangible possessions. Quite to the contrary, I hold that man too often subjects himself to the Tyranny of Things. It seems to me that the prime reason for man's labor is far beyond the battle for food and shelter. We live fully only when we attend to the needs of the spirit, and aspire to a creative life. The acquisition of Things, necessary to a minimal point, is thereafter valueless compared to curiosity concerning the mysteries of nature. In these terms man has a capacity for which energy, whether the burning of wood, the falling of water, or the severing of an atom, are nothing more than tools. They are never the end, but only a means—slaves, not masters—serfs, not gods.

Above all, I have long felt that given our soil, varied climates, rich chemicals and hidden mineral deposits, the only difference between creating a full life of the spirit and a meager vegetating life of the body lies in what we do to the mind and imagination of our people. This concept leads to certain assumptions. First and foremost, that no matter what wars will be fought in the coming decades, they will leave waste and havoc of no more than a reparable type. The atom will not be employed to murder civilizations. Second, we are experiencing a different kind of world where the new slaves of man called "energies" will be employed so that no longer will man live under the compulsion of spending most of his hours in the dreary and increasingly uncreative scramble for sustenance or the building of shelter. Third, as our new energies continue to reduce the personal joys man historically has found in solitary or joint uses of hand skills, we will substitute the greater creative satisfactions to be found in our leisure time as we change from an audience society to a fully participating culture. Then our people will become critical as well as literate.

Of course I run the risk of being proven wrong in 1976. But the falsity of my prophecies will not rest on the figures and facts, nor be because my dreams are fantastically impossible. Other people also have dreams, and some even dream of the destruction of civilization. In addition, we must recognize the most dangerous—those who do not dream at all. Even if the pessimistic dream is defeated, the nondreamers may prevent any Utopia. Dreams are a form of ideas and hence are powerful makers of history. Nineteen seventy-six is of course not ineluctably determined in 1955, but here I write the story as I see it and as it will be—if enough men and women so want it.

Chapter 2

OUR NEW LEISURE AND
ITS GOOD USES

THE BASIS OF THIS CHAPTER IS THE INFLEXIBLE NUMBER 168.
There are only 168 hours in a week. About a third of these
are presently needed for sleep. This figure may be much
reduced as we approach the less tense and more satisfying
way of living of 1976. Experiments indicate that under
relaxed and satisfying habits six hours will be enough to
replenish our body energies. But on the basis of eight
hours of sleep, fifty-six hours a week, we have about 112
hours left for work, eating and play.

In 1776 the work portion amounted to 80 hours.

In 1900, 60 hours.

In 1925, 50 hours.

In 1933, 47 hours.

In 1953, 40 hours for all but farmers, who work 52
hours.

In 1976 the work portion will amount to 30 hours or less.

During the eighteenth century there was slight change in the number of hours of labor needed to keep man alive. In a later chapter I deal with the new magic sources of energy and electronics which in the future will more than double our national output while we all work fewer hours. Labor will be replaced manifold by the machine, giving us two hours additional each day for pleasure, or what is correctly termed re-creation. Ownership of time will be as satisfying as ownership of land, and give more pleasure than possession of things.

The rate of increased leisure-time frightens many. It should not, however, surprise anyone who was an adult before 1933. Such folk have seen the change and have enjoyed the shift from travail to relaxation. The five-day week was a revolutionary invention. In our own lifetime major American industries were tied up by strikes because workers demanded a forty-eight-hour work week, or Saturdays off. The six-hour day, five-day week, deemed unconscionable at the turn of the century, has already touched many industrial occupations, while farmers worked eight hours less a week in 1954 than they did in 1933.

Of course not every twenty years hereafter will bring a similar shift from labor to fun. Obviously the rate of shift must decline since if it were not so, then by the year 2000 we would live lives of plenty without any work at all. However, during the next score of years we may come close to the peak of the pace-change from work to leisure. The use of the new energies, coupled with electronic and automatic controls, fortunately or unfortunately will take pleasure out of most work. By 1976 only those who deal in ideas, carry on research and make the new machines will get creative pleasure from their work hours. The rest of mankind will seek the creative equivalents in their uses of leisure.

We are often limited in our thinking by the changing content of words. "Work" is less than precise in its connotations. Some is pleasure-giving—some is a bore. Work is more fun for some than leisure is for others. "Leisure" is also an unprecise and hence misleading word. For a long time it was related to mortal sin, and generally deemed a peril for the mass of mankind. Even today it is a meager way to describe the hours man has available for other purposes than maintaining his physical existence. We must forget the ancient and dishonorable derivation of the word "leisure" which, from the Latin *licere*, means to "let," or to "allow." For centuries leisure was no more than a permitted or inherited way of life. It was a privilege and not a right. Our historic battle cry of independence talked about Pursuit of Happiness, but in that era happiness for the masses was to be obtained mainly by work for the production of wealth.

Through the ages, most men and women were too busy answering the stern demands of the belly to spend waking hours other than in pursuit of the harsh necessities of survival. On the other hand, the rich lived, often and intentionally, in ways far removed from production, trade or commerce. They were the playboys, not the workers. As a class, they employed their leisure as a symbol of snobbery, typified by such fruitless pursuits as fox-hunting or falconry, conscious symbols of conspicuous expenditure of time. Most religious creeds abetted the urgent drive of mankind to work and work and work for food and shelter. This, to be sure, was in most climes and cultures a necessary rule of survival economics, unfortunately promoted into a moral dogma. Even today those who enjoy leisure are seldom disturbed about its abuses by their own class but seem to be much worried about the harm that leisure will do to others!

At many times in history a small cultured leisure class made great contributions. Our own Republic could scarcely have been founded with its inventive societal concepts if it had not been for the Founding Fathers who, in a land of illiterates, expressed the highest form of governmental vision evidenced by man. We owe a debt to them as we do also to such leisuremen as the Medici, the patrons of Leonardo da Vinci. The Renaissance was nourished by a very small leisure class to whom we still give thanks. Increasingly, however, leisure has become a democratic way of life. It seems clear to me that wisely handled we will find in our land by 1976 much presently unlocated genius. Our people will fail to attain a new renaissance only if they fear leisure and fail to discard their ingrained sense of guilt toward it. This attitude of guilt was encouraged by the leisure class so successfully that until recently the ever working masses sneered at the so-called idle" rich. Furthermore, the churchmen, in their desire to teach the value of work habits, put a kind of social curse on leisure for the masses.

This helped make life simpler if not more leisurely, as life always is simpler the fewer choices we have. Many of us have even come to like it that way. Thousands of boys in the army decline appointments as officers because they fear the responsibility of decision-making. They do not know that the spirit of man is enriched to the degree that he is presented with choices and elects his own values.

In 1780 one of our historic leisurists, Benjamin Franklin, wrote to Joseph Priestley: "The rapid progress true science now makes, occasions my regretting sometimes that I was born too soon. It is impossible to imagine the height to which may be carried in a thousand years the power of men over matter. We may perhaps learn to deprive large masses of their gravity and give them absolute levity, for the sake of easy transport. Agriculture may diminish its labor and double its produce; all diseases may be by sure means prevented or cured, not excepting even that of age, and our lives lengthened at pleasure even beyond the antediluvian standard. O, that a moral science were in a fair way of improvement that men would cease to be wolves to one another, and that human beings would at length learn what they now improperly call humanity."

When I first looked at how America spends its leisure, my mind went to the watching of television, watching baseball, watching movies, and watching theater. The facts I found are a welcome shock. Our people are already shifting with great speed from an audience society to a participating society.

Of course, readers of good will may differ as to the meaning of "participation." I make no firm dichotomy, even of an academic nature, between audience and participating uses of time. Reading, for example, may be rather passive, but it is likely to create mental activity—by an association with the characters in a book or by the emotional or intellectual pursuit of the forces depicted by the author. Obviously, participating of a sort exists in television viewing or radio listening, the latter even when driving a car. The housewife at her sewing machine creating a new garment can use her handicraft skill while also imbibing a Toscanini program. The spectrum from imbibing to doing is a vast one with indefinable gradations. So I depict our present and future scene only in terms of broad but strong general trends.

The do-it-yourself market invited three and a half billions of consumer dollars in the year 1954. Thirty-five million of us spent forty-five million dollars for classical-music concerts while thirty-seven million attended major- and minor-league baseball games, paying only forty million dollars for tickets. The flower-seed and potted-plant industry is close to one billion dollars this year, and will soon exceed the total admission paid in all our theaters and movies, which in 1952 totaled a little more than 1,200 million dollars. Our classical-record business is more than 24 per cent of all record sales, and totals more than sixty million dollars. We have at present more than twenty million music students, over one thousand writers on musical topics and nearly a thousand symphony orchestras. Nearly one hundred organizations of so-called lay persons interested in music total a membership of sixty thousand. By 1976 each town will have its quartets and each city its orchestra.

The musical revival is already on its way. In a decade, electronic music will be in full use and man's experimentation in the field of pleasure through hearing will result in more than passing fads. People will play more and maybe listen less. Ours will be an enriched culture when millions play their own music rather than listen to expert performances. This kind of group behavior pattern will expand, particularly as our middle-class women abandon some of those vicarious leisure habits established by Mrs. Jones. We may even revert to group dancing—the original art form for body motion in time with music.

The competitive aspects of music or the dance will no doubt continue, and will be valuable in terms of creating standards of what our society in 1976 will declare, tentatively, to be perfection. The values of such competition will be quite unlike the present aspects of the need for notoriety by a people who, starved creatively, require vicarious identification with the so-called successful. People will prefer to spend for a new violin or piano rather than for a mink coat—the latter becoming a badge of women who are inwardly unsatisfied, or of men who need the kudos of showing how well they can dress their wives.

While the money spent on newspaper advertising of sporting goods increased from one and one-half million in 1948 to two and one-half in 1953, the advertising of jewelry declined in the same years from $1,610,000 to $1,170,000. In a random check of ten suburban communities, 94 per cent of the men were Mr. Fixits, and 8 per cent owned "work" clothes. Mind you, this is not the same as sport clothes. Programs are already on the air giving the audience instructions in woodworking, paper hanging and painting, and in electrical and even plumbing projects. Before widespread leisure, work clothes were for men in mines, on farms, or in factories. In 1976 home-work clothes will be used generally by all people of all ages.

In 1929 the purchase of pets—take your choice between this leisure occupation as audience or participating —was about twenty-five million dollars; the same in 1939; but sixty million in 1952. The money we spend on dogs exceeds the total personal income of the entire population of Vermont. By 1976, this substitute outlet for affection, domination, or company, is likely to diminish as loneliness declines.

Fishing is like and unlike having a pet—unlike in its murderous objective, but similar in its setting which invites pondering on the habits and oddities of other forms of life. Both occupations in fact are at times inducive to great contemplation. The amount spent on deep-sea fishing in Florida is greater than the combined grosses of that state's citrus and cattle industries. More than eighteen million fresh-water and seven million salt-water fishing licenses were issued last year. Thirty-five million dollars was spent for the licenses alone, a sum in excess of the money spent for hand lotions and creams, and nearly as much as the sum spent on stomach sweeteners. Moreover, much of the fishing is from boats—an industry until recently considered to be in the luxury class. We own five million pleasure boats used by seventeen million people and over twenty thousand of our pleasure craft are in a newly created body of water, the TVA watershed. This is no exclusive seaside sport. More pleasure boats are registered with the U.S. Coast Guard at St. Louis than in Boston. It is estimated that over 200,000 people are building their own boats at this moment in their cellars or barns. In fact, one mail-order house ordered forty thousand boat kits, each to be put together into an assembler's dream ship. I have seen estimates of as many as fifty million boats in 1976, with an increase in outboard motors (now self-starting and silent) from the present four and a half million to a minimum of twenty-five million. For some odd reason—maybe because our census takers are not yet aware of the revolution in our leisure habits—the rental of boats is often coupled with the renting of bicycles, which, with repairs, was tabulated as an eight-million-dollar business in 1939, growing to more than double that figure in 1952. With the increase of boat trailers, by 1976 three quarters of our families may own boats.

Photography intrigues thirty-five million amateurs and fifty-five thousand professionals, who own over sixty million cameras. In the last two decades amateur photographers nearly tripled in number, and cameras quadrupled. Photography is a billion-dollar industry. More Americans, in fact, have cameras than telephones, and some estimates indicate that of the amateurs with cameras five million are "serious" and two million are expert. It would be my guess that photography will decline as painting, etching and water-color work increases, except for those photographers who develop and print their own product.

Indoor games of skill use up much of our time and dollars. Billiards, pool and bowling cost about sixty million dollars in 1929. In 1954 it came to 130 million. Tennis claims seven million adherents, professional gardeners eighteen million, bird watchers over eight million, and so the story goes.

There are more than 250,000 radio hams, more than 500,000 model airplane buffs. The collecting instinct satisfies millions who gather stones, shells, stamps, butterflies, coffee spoons, baby shoes, et cetera, and one company sold four million antique-auto kits last year. Coloring pictures by numbers in 1952 drew thirty-five million dollars from our leisure pocketbooks, and it is estimated that 10 per cent of those who buy ready-to-paint sets graduate to painting on their own.

One of the most striking items is the registration at public libraries for a twelve-week college course on the uses of leisure—captioned in one of our dailies as "How to Loaf Artistically." No one can be unaware of the advertisements in most of our magazines and newspapers of "Where to Put Your Power Tools"—a business which grew from seven million dollars in 1947 to 150 million dollars in 1953. One fifth of all our homes—that is over ten million—have carpentry shops with some kind of power tool. Over 50 per cent of all paint sold for home use is put on by the occupant himself. Wallpaper manufacturers and plywood producers are fully aware of this new trend. Not to mention the growth of power lawn mowers for home use from 10,000 in 1945 to 1,400,000, in 1953.

Emerson wrote: "The crowning fortune of a man is to be born to some pursuit which finds him employment and happiness, whether it be to make baskets, or broadswords, or canals or statues or songs."

In Emerson's day there was no leisure time—except for the rich—and even in 1909 only 3 per cent of all consumer expenditures were on recreation. By 1953 this percentage was doubled on a vastly increased income and population.

Our mores are becoming less tense and, despite outward appearances, many homes are finding resources for greater relaxation. Certainly this is true in uncongested areas, and may be one of the real social causes for dispersal from the large cities to the suburbs and the countryside. Such dispersal is often further induced by economic advantages to the employer who wisely sees a more productive environment for his workers if they can save travel time from portal to portal. But beyond this, the worker finds increasing difficulty in buying anything he deems of value with the extra dollars paid in the big centers of population. On top of this, the surtax theory of our income taxes tends to narrow the gap in take-home pay after taxes, between the larger wage paid in the big city and the lesser sum paid outside of metropolitan areas.

But the chief item of inducement toward plant dispersal is that the worker finds leisure outlets outside of the metropolis more varied and far less costly. In a big city there is scant opportunity to respond to the advertised appeals of "Place your workbench in your cellar," or "You can easily construct a camera darkroom out of plywood." Apartments are not equipped for the use of our greatly increased leisure.

The result is that the young engineer in Maine earning six thousand dollars cannot easily be induced to shift his job to Chicago or New York City for three times the salary. Quite properly he suggests that Uncle Sam gets a goodly hunk of the extra twelve thousand dollars. And then he asks, "But what do I buy in the big city with the extra take-home pay?" In Maine, the ski run and the mooring for his home-built boat are all within a half hour by car. His wife walks across some fields to take the kids to school. A barn or extra room is available for the hobbies of father, mother and the children.

As we take away the need for skills in work and hence remove the satisfactions of creative outlets from more of our people, the pressure for creative activity in the leisure hours or days becomes increasingly urgent. It has been suggested that there may well be a correlation between ulcers and the bottling up of urban leisure desires. I do not suggest that we will develop new human facilities as a result of released time for fun, but certainly the surge of amateur gardening (home gardeners now raise one sixth of all our home-eaten vegetables) may well be the outlet for a genuine affinity to the soil—a human drive suppressed except in the case of farmers. I suggest that people will live better when closer to green land, the sight of clouds and a sense of stars and wind. Living outside of congested areas produces a kind of antidote to the obvious fast aging of those who live surrounded by unhappy and unfulfilled lives. This kind of happiness may not be inheritable but certainly can be passed on, since children learn most effectively from observation and imitation. There is a kind of fellowship within hobbies, a kinship of leisure occupations which apparently is far more vital than the fellowship of the discontented on which totalitarianism and dictatorships always have thrived.

In our land, as we moved in our westward trek and replaced personal skills with machines, comradeship became a tenuous thing. Rotary Clubs, Elks and numberless fraternal organizations were created to satisfy our desires to "belong." We were a lonely people in this period of our history.

We were restless, too. Two and a half million trailers used as homes, thirty thousand hotels and twenty-five thousand motels are indications of the domestic travel industry's magnitude. It has its counterpart in the lure of other lands. In 1949 we spent about $1,600,000,000 on foreign travel, in 1952 more than $2,250,000,000 (exclusive of that spent by the government for moving its civilian and military personnel abroad). Such use of leisure has staggering implications. When Galileo saw a new world in his telescope he experienced a change of vision not unlike that which happens to the hundreds of thousands of our citizens who travel for the first time outside their own local frames of reference.

To cross the man-made boundaries of nations and cultures causes discoveries of inner richness of enduring nature. The traveler to a "foreign" culture—from Cutler, Maine, to Natchez, Mississippi, or from Jersey City to Rome—incorporates within himself fertile areas for future imaginings and comparative judgments. The wayfarer abandons some of his circumscribed notions of a finiteness of life—no matter where his home port may be. The mysteries and varieties of man's failure, or ability, to adapt to his environment is often the springboard for the satisfactions he can get from traveling standing still. Literature, art and the potential comradeship of the human race can rise to unimaginable heights of understanding. Contemplations become enriched and the age-old concept of sin of physical inactivity is diminished. The dreams of the loafer are surely full of motion and travel.

As distinguished from the democratization of leisure travel—learning by seeing instead of by reading—additional nonwork hours will also provide a quite different source of happiness. Maybe the greatest of joys are private. Seeing a star, hearing a bird, becoming aware of a flower, sensing a new smell, touching an old piece of carved wood. These are the joys of leisure experienced one by one, perhaps two by two, but not in a group.

By 1976 the dead level of orthodoxy imposed during work periods will be offset by its decrease in leisure hours. Invention—since our people are overwhelmingly gadgeteers—will bloom in our new leisure as never before as we ride our hobbies, unafraid of being submerged by the prestige pressures of cultural and group patterns. The spirit of 1776, symbolized by the amateur architect Jefferson and the amateur electrical engineer Franklin, will by 1976 spread all through our culture.

Our horizons will be broadened as we travel by millions—a week end in Morocco or Alaska replacing the present week end in Bermuda. Libraries and museums will increase so that we will not have to look with envy on Scandinavian and Lowland cultures, nor see our own unwholesomely bottlenecked in New York, Washington and one or two other centers. Museums of art and natural history will ship vast collections out on circuit tours. Dozens of new private special collections will be set up in small, medium and large cities.

Since books are the instruments of continuity, our reading habits will undergo a revolution. We will know that reading too little may delay the process of growing up, and lead to an addiction to a literary diet of an extreme escapist nature. We will realize fully that so-called "bad" books do not create delinquency. We will see clearly that the boy who reads about climbing Mt. Everest is less likely to be influenced by horror comics or daily tabloid sadism than the lad who has not read about exciting struggles against nature.

Radio and television will no doubt continue to be part of an effortless imbibing, but the difficulty of supplying over five billion new words a year to fill our demanding ether may well create a competitive disability, as compared to the more qualitative and less quantitative appeals for man's leisure. In fact, the so-called hobby occupations will often arouse compulsion drives in excess of the first compulsive use of television a few years ago. With radio and television programs determined on the basis of the willingness of consumers to pay directly therefor, the product will improve and become tuned to our new attitudes toward leisure. In a sense, radio may still meet with favor as a background emission while the home audience is painting, sewing, weaving or doing homemaking chores.

What kind of television or radio will be needed to compete against the interests of the young teen-agers who build a Wilson Cloud chamber to see cosmic rays? These now ill-directed pipe lines to the home will have to adjust to the high school children who build cyclotrons, construct a pottery kiln, or fabricate a useful planetarium. Such are the unusual of 1955—but their counterparts will be the ordinary of 1976.

In the meantime, attendance at sports will decline, compared to the growth of the more give-to-it pastimes.

There are present signs that athletic attendance is less satisfying to our new ways of living than do-it-yourself bowling, skating, swimming, skiing or sailing. Horseshoe pitching is by no means finished as a skill to test man's co-ordinations of mind and arm. In the main the trend appears to be in the direction of those arts and pleasures which call for collaboration or contest with nature rather than with man.

Man has always needed an outlet for his creative libido—a far more salutory catharsis than thriving on misery in the lives of others. The clothes, furniture and furnishings we will create for ourselves will have values far richer than those of the purchased items. What we make will include part of ourselves. Nor is it an answer for the supercilious, by facile comparison to the creations of a Leonardo da Vinci, to deplore the mass attempts to raise our level of taste and beauty. Who knows but that among the women who paint for fun one may not be our first female Van Dyke?

Genius is not created. It is discovered in a ripe environment. It can be encouraged and recognized far better in a society in which many have tried their hand at the arts. The very act of trying will add to the discrimination of our people. Thus, even if the new democratization of an art should develop no additional genius, it will certainly help all who struggle with a medium better to judge the achievement of the extraordinary. Nineteen seventy-six will not create genius, but will detect it with greater ease and in greater numbers. I do not believe genius thrives only in attics of starvation, or that just because Schubert never had a piece of music paper and lined every scrap he could find, that all men of exceptional ear should have no lined paper. Nineteen seventy-six will at least explode the myth that the exquisite joy given to millions by genius could be created only in suffering and misery.

The skill of one adult in a family will touch off the lives of the entire group, and especially through the fingers and eyes of the unsophisticated children will come increased beauty and form. In a rich culture, among a contented nonbelligerent people, it is less important to have a few of us reach the so-called top rung of the ladder than to have the median of all people constantly climbing to a higher step on the ladder.

The intensity of the hobbyist will surprise our historians. Hours, mealtime and sleep mean little when man is creating. Nor does such intensity seem excessively to drain off energy. The creatively happy apparently need less sleep and wake up with eagerness in the morning, anxious to face a new day of adventure. Boredom, like the hum of the motor, induces sleep. Creation seems to build energy and not consume it, as does lethargy. A sign of the mentally ill is their lack of creative desires, their failure to be satisfied. The lad who hangs around the street corner may need more sleep than does the intensely interested ham radio operator.

One novel impression is seen in our games. (Card playing is difficult to appraise for although it attracts a vast part of our public, the attraction is more often related to winning money than to the esteem that comes from successful skill.) The recent shift of a literate people to word games is best seen in the crossword puzzles carried in newspapers throughout the land. This new sort of leisure play has profound implications. It will lead to further enrichment of our vocabularies, and by 1976 may bring into its own the thrilling adventure of the study of etymology. For the mentally alert the origin of words not only adds to the subtleties of reading and speech but may well lead to a much-needed approach to the learning of other tongues, ancient or living. Before 1976 foreign languages will enter into such games.

The tramper in the woods, the flycaster in the stream, the amateur astronomer or even the casual sailor, belong to those who are aware of the mysteries of life. A blade of grass is seen pushing through the macadam road. Who is to say that observing it shows less awareness of the power of an unseen force than the singing of a liturgy?

Increasingly, man is less interested in the fires of hell than in an electric stove in his home, and the music of the angels in heaven does not sound as clear as a Toscanini-led orchestra. I think that over the next few decades man will learn to live life for life's sake, with less regard for the honey of heaven or the tortures of hell.

Outside of the family we will have time to cooperate with community groups for the common welfare. The urge of our people to join parent-teachers, taxpayers, and other associations is only at its inception. The matrix of our communal existence by 1976 will have shifted from elected officials to many millions of people united in a common purpose for the better park, playground, sewer system, or art gallery of their city. Our communities will be effective because of local pride, a "concern" in the Quaker sense of the word. Above all, this enjoyable use of leisure will reinvigorate our ten thousand weekly newspapers (the national magazines have little impact on local problems and local life). Vast additional leisure time will make possible the contribution of hours and energy, formerly supplied only by a few lucky rich, for the benefit of their communities.

Not only will we own time for living, but our increased productivity will increase the tools to enrich life. We will become awake to new capacities of man. Then we will face an Age of Pericles, not ordained by a dictator, but blossoming from the might of millions of our people understanding themselves and their potentials for a rich full life through leisure—the end purpose of all forms of energy.

Chapter 3

OUR NEW BENEFACTORS

WE ARE AT THE END OF AN ERA—A SHORT BUT VIOLENT ONE. Violent in the sense that the income and comforts of our people changed more during the past 188 years than in all the previous history of man. The changes which occurred in 188 years were more profound than in hundreds of thousands of years of man's adventure on his earth. They occurred because man had an idea. The idea was steam and the momentous year was 1767. There was nothing very new about steam, but for centuries no one had known how to make use of it. Steam's immediate heir, electricity, accelerated the revolution. The idea of steam power was recorded as early as 300 B.C. and although the concept was precise at that time, nevertheless its application was a secret from all men.

A century ago our annual per capita income in present dollars was about $320. Steam and electricity brought it to more than $1,500 in constant dollars. The lowest estimates for 1964 bring us to $2,000 per capita, and by 1976, with the atom split for our convenience, our annual income will equal more than $4,000 per capita for every man, woman and child of our lucky Republic. This means a total national income rising from 250 billion dollars (electric) today, to a minimum of 800 billion dollars (fission and solar) in 1976. For our 190 million population of 1976 the benefactions of the new energies may even bring us to a trillion dollars gross national product in present values, or $25,000 per family. Only lack of vision and wisdom can prevent that seemingly improbable level.

Man has reverted to a variation of that ancient dream of two thousand years ago when the alchemist toyed with the mutation of elements into gold. Within the last decade man seized that idea and was wise enough to bend it for his own use. We are inside a new age. Power from the breakup of matter in existence around us for aeons will be released in units so small as to be invisible to the human eye. The atomic age in twenty years will create more changes than steam and electricity produced in their 188 years. We will produce more in the next ten years than we have in the past hundred. Let us not be brash and talk with finalities, for this is not to be man's last adventure with energy, even though it is our present special treasure. More and better energies will come via some dreaming poet of nature. Nor should anyone deny that this is to be the age of most radical departure from human physical effort ever experienced by man. The buggy is closer to the most modern auto than is electric to atomic power.

One need not understand the properties of the vacuum tube to enjoy the radio. We may know less about aerodynamics than did Icarus, but we will ride the rocket plane for a week-end visit to any town on our earth. Smoothly and quickly man takes inventiveness for granted. For man is a tool-using animal. Without tools he amounts to little.

For millions of years man was the buffet of cruel nature, his greatest enemy. He had to tame nature, growing food and building protections against cold. Only after these victories, which took thousands of years of perpetual and exclusive effort, were his other advances accelerated. The lever, the centerboard and the round wheel were early tools derived from an attitude of kindly cooperation with nature.

It is significant that more than a quarter of the intake of man's energy goes to the brain; an enormous consumption in relation to the size and weight of that tiny organ. The deep wells of unconscious cerebration are the core of man's future, and energy consumed therein is clearly man's best investment. As Sir Francis Bacon prophesied in his *New Atlantis,* 1624, "the end of our foundation is the knowledge of causes and of the secret of things," and we are soon to adopt the position that the future of man stems from the men of speculation whose trade is not to do anything but to observe everything. The flashes and leaps of the human mind are paying off. If the history of man is represented by twenty-four hours, only the last thirty seconds cover man's episode with science.

A concept of the steam engine "hit" the mind of Watt on the way "to the golf house," in 1767. Not unrelated to this "hit," the output of coal in Britain rose from half a ton a head in 1700 to three tons a head in 1850. From 1850 to 1910 the world's coal consumption increased from 50 to 1,000 million tons a year, while the world's railroads grew from 25,000 to 600,000 miles. In our land alone we have 230,000 miles of railroads. One energy replaces another. The first oil well in Pittsburgh in 1859 was insignificant compared to man's new insight into basic relations of matter and energy—the X ray, the electron, the nucleus, the quantum theory and relativity.

We have invented no new energies. We have not even discovered them. They were recognized or discerned centuries ago. However, we have domesticated them and they are to be the new friends, allies and servants of all people of the earth.

The history of man can be measured in terms of his use of sources of energy and his search for new sources. His first was wood, but the more progressive societies soon realized the limitations of the forests. The Babylonian Empire (2500 to 538 B.C.) used asphalt and crude petroleum. The Chinese were mining coal in 1100 B.C. and using natural gas for space heating and lighting. The Phoenicians learned how to use the energy of the wind for sailing their vessels. With the coming of Confucianism in China and the downfall of the Babylonian Empire, technological progress halted, and, with the denuding of the forests, many parts of the world came near to disaster. It was the Greek interest in empirical as well as abstract thought that prepared for the kind of scientific inquiry that has made our world possible.

Whale oil was our principal source of light until 1850, when the whale population dangerously declined. Kerosene and natural gas appeared as a replacement for a half century. But the great need of the world was for a new fuel to supply the new industrialization. Across Nantucket Sound from where I write, on Cape Cod, the forests supported a dozen important industries in 1800. By 1900, with the forests gone, towns of 12,000 became villages of 1,000. Industries closed down. People moved to areas where they could find employment. Of all the fossil fuel recovered since the earth was created, 86 per cent has been used since 1900. All the fossil fuel consumed in the world up to 1900 would satisfy the present world requirements for no more than five years. Only a short time ago, about sixteen times as much power energy arose from the muscle of man and beast as from fossil fuels. Today this relationship is reversed.

We can already see the outlines of the 1976 products. Telephone and telegraph lines are to give way to microwave radio. Electronic lighting will give safety on sea and land. Atomic batteries are not far off. A solar battery now exists for man to see. New industries in our land will be located for the convenience of people and will not have to be adjacent to a supply of coal, oil or fall of water. An inch cube of fission fuel even today will yield as much power as 1,500 tons of coal. Travel by air, by boat and by car will rely on atomic fission. In fact, we will have wide choices among what were the original ninety-two elements. The insignificance of its dimensions adds to the glory of our newest wealth-giving ally. My own appreciation of the extent of the power of the physical though unseeable was first made clear when I saw a blade of grass push its way up through an asphalt country road. Then I bowed to the greatness of the tiny and the slow moving. The worship of the giant in any sphere implies that man looks through the wrong end of life's telescope. A microscopic weed possesses more strength than the toolless arm of the biggest man.

The results of our scientific advances will pervade our lives. Foods will be sterilized by split-second exposures, thus extending the shelf life of fresh foods practically indefinitely. Fission rays will immunize seeds, oats and other grains against disease. Doctors will substitute new agents for ancient drugs. Clothing will be produced impervious to stain, unmussable and durable for the lives of consumers. Plastics subjected to atomic radiation will develop new characteristics such as resistance to steam. Autos of plastic will last for decades, and tires will show no ill effects of use. Bathtubs and home equipment made of plastic will weigh so little that a child will be able to lift them. Plastic boats, and houses made with plastic adhesions will require no nails. Man will make substitutes for fur and leather. As yet our chemists and metallurgists have toyed with less than a third of the known metals. Titanium is already with us—tough as steel, a third the weight, and the earth's fourth most common metal. If we need iron ore in 1976 we will extract it from available taconite rock. Our paint bill will be eliminated by smokeless power and nontarnishing and nonfading materials.

I do not say that each and every one of these adventures of physicists and chemists will be in common use before 1976. They will be available, and those not yet commercially arrived will be delayed around the corner only because we do not yet want them. Possibly we may want something else—say leisure—more than we want new, different or additional things. But the plastic-domed house with glass walls and plastic panels, plastic floors with ducts for air conditioning, and curtains of light between rooms is on the drawing boards for 1964.

Leading engineers predict fission will be cheaper than coal—an equivalent, before 1960, of six dollars a ton for coal. A packaged atomic reactor with easy mobility, sufficient to light a community of 15,000 and supply all its industry, is around the corner in England.

The moth will look for its diet elsewhere than in the clothes closet. Bugs and shrill noises will be barricaded from us by chemically treated paints, materials and electronics. The regulation of climate will greatly enhance our production. Let the skeptic take note that an eighty-room house has long been heated in Hartwell, England, by atomically generated heat. The heat generated by radioactive decay at this one experiment saves one and a half million gallons of fuel annually. Coventry Cathedral is being reconstructed with pinky gray sandstone similar to the stone used in the original historic structure, and in the prospectus we read that the new heating plant will be convertible from oil to fission.

Electric power now costs, at the point of creation in the United States, two to eight mills per kilowatt-hour. The most conservative of authorities—the kind that always protects its reputation for caution—admits that nuclear power will be below such cost before 1976. In 1932 we had only 100 billion of national kilowatt-hours. At the close of 1951 this stood at about 430 billion kilowatt-hours. By 1976—who knows the figure! With the new energy the rate of growth will be greater than over the two decades, 1932-1952.

Lest the reader still be cynical, I shall refer to a few basic facts of some of the present and future energies.

Our fossil-fuel supply may last until 1976, but scarcely beyond that date if our desires are to be, as I suspect they will be, for material things that require energy for creation. The total production of energy from mineral fuels, oil, natural gas, water power and wood increased our per capita consumption of electricity from 455 kw-h. in 1924 to about 3,000 kw-h. in 1954. Many authorities, viewing these old-fashioned sources, conceive of an increase of only 50 per cent over fifty years, or one per cent a year, an increase which would admittedly not keep pace with our rising population and desires.

The use of oil will increase for some time. We have

produced over forty billion barrels and our reserves are somewhere between thirty and sixty billion more. But we used about two billion barrels in 1950. Costs of oil discovery, originally fifteen cents per barrel, are already sixty cents and may well go beyond a dollar. We may even convert coal to oil rather than distill oil from crude petroleum.

With decreasing petroleum supplies, the demand for coal is expected to rise by about 50 per cent by 1976, and coal may recover outlets lost to oil because of the previous visionless operations of coal companies. Coal if used at all will be gassified underground, with pipe-line transmission as a gas or liquid. With its by-products of sulphur in one spot in one state, oil shale could yield many billions of barrels of liquid fuel this year at a market price of only two cents a gallon above gasoline.

I like to think that the discovery of the use of water to do man's work originated in the mind of a child. The guileless and unsophisticated often first glimpse the importance in the simplest events of nature. It is most likely that a child discovered the round wheel while playing or helping his father with a circular stone or a stump, and a fishing adolescent, wanting to get home against the wind, used his slab of oarwood as the first outrigger, centerboard or keel, without which our travel would still be subservient to the directions chosen by current and wind. Harnessed water became the magnet for clusters of people. Of the world's existing water power, about 100 million horsepower, we have about one quarter. World sur-

veys estimate the existence of an undeveloped amount of
six or seven times that quantity. That which we have built,
kindly TVA, is justly one of our most famed historic
monuments. Its power is fabulous, the pattern it set for
the world is thrilling, and what it did to the lives of
millions of people in the Valley is the story for which
Senator Norris and President Roosevelt may still get their
greatest recognition in history.

Many people are troubled about the shortage of our
water potentials. To be sure, Russia and other nations
have more falling water reserves than we have. One of the
hard facts that man must face is that 94 per cent of the
world's coal and 83 per cent of the world's oil lie north
of the 20° latitude—that is, the Havana, Mecca, Formosa
parallel, while two thirds of the earth's water power lies
to the south of that line. In our climate, approximately
70 per cent of the water that falls returns to the atmosphere; the balance seeks streams and rivers, or remains
under the soil above the water table. A high proportion
of the people of our nation still dig wells to provide a
major part of the water they need, and we dare not over-
look the billions of gallons pumped from below to irrigate
our fields, even though today this is only a small part of
the total irrigation water. With weather and rain control,
this figure will be what we care to make it, for with
chemical farming, water will be a stretchable commodity.
In fact, the thirty-inch mean rainfall in the United States
adds up to a daily gift from above of over 4,000 billion
gallons of water a day. Water purification from salt, or

what are today contaminated streams, will take care of much of our drinking water problem. With the dispersal from big cities, no longer will the people of a metropolis have to go two hundred miles through tunnels and by under-river syphons for a glass of drinking water, as the inhabitants of New York City do today. Maybe in the future, the size of a community will be limited by two factors: the optimum decent size of a school population, and the water supply available for personal, industrial and agricultural uses.

The cost of irrigation and industrial water will surely be cut in half—a saving sufficient to let every person have a sailboat, allow our scientists to research to death the common cold or permit all our cities to build libraries and put on their shelves thousands of books.

The vast capital we now have and will wisely put into public dams, for power and pleasure purposes, will repay their cost by 1976 when the new energies will supplant as we see fit the more expensive and less mobile present sources of energy. For the time being, much of the water power may be married to fission power.

Now let us look at some of the new sources which lie just around the corner of man's mind:

Chlorella, discussed elsewhere as a nutriment, can be carbonized to produce coal and be transformed into gasoline. At present the conversion cost takes it out of the market, but some scientists leave chlorella in the spectrum of 1966-76 fuels.

Solar energy: all the heat and power now consumed

in our land could be produced from the sun on an area of about 50,000 square miles at about 440,000 horsepower per acre per annum. Plants use practically none of the sun's radiation in photosynthesis. At the start we will have to select cloudless regions of low latitude for our solar energy, even though these regions up to now have not supported our greatest industrial complexes. Already, one house in Boston, with large windows, has flat plate solar collectors and an insulated body of water for heat storage. Solar energy contributed over 80 per cent of the total heating load of that home. India has a Solar Cooker, weighing 30 pounds, with a heating capacity of a 400-watt electric oven, price $16.80, no cost to operate and usable about 300 days a year. One great authority estimates that one fifth of the total comfort heating load (that is, 6 per cent of our total energy system) will be carried by this gift from the sun.

If the rest of the world today were using all known sources of energy at the rate of our own consumption, the world's present known mineral fuels would be expended in less than a week. But the sun gives us at least thirty thousand times as much energy as all the fuel and water power now used. Even pessimists will agree that the sun will rise and set for quite a while. Only a few will doom its dispensation of heat before 1976, and still fewer will discount science's march to harness the sun at rates commercially competitive with nuclear fission and most of our old-fashioned friends.

But if you grant the sun, then you must also concede

me the winds, for their relationship is not remote. In the last decade, thousands of pumping windmills were sold annually in our land. Our windpower generators produce billions of kilowatt-hours a year. For understandable reasons our trend of wind use has been downward, but Denmark has about eighty-eight wind-powered generators in commercial use, and Russia claims a 5,000-kilowatt wind turbine. Wind energy is presently limited to areas with rather steady eighteen to twenty-five-mile winds, and Great Britain is looking toward a 100-kilowatt wind unit replacing four million tons of coal a year. Wind is an old source, but with the magic of our new sciences it may surprise us all.

Another old challenge is the inexhaustible tide that rolls as the earth turns over. Someone figured out that the loss of kinetic energy by the earth as it slows down (about one second per thousand years) equals the continuous dissipation of two billion horsepower—about one half of the present world consumption. There are not many sites for tidal transformation, but Passamaquoddy may still supply the Eastern seaboard. In that bay one woodsaw is now turned by tide, just as at the old London Bridge a tide wheel in 1824 supplied water-pumping power. The amount of water flowing daily in and out of the Fundy Bay equals a sixty-two-mile cube of water. It's hard for me to believe that we won't domesticate a little bit of it.

I like these gifts of the inexhaustible, and so I also put in your mind natural steam, escaping from fissures in rocks, already used in Iceland, California and especially

in Tuscany where one plant produces millions of kilowatt-
hours a year.

However, our problem is no longer one of energy,
but rather of what to do with its fruits. What kind of
lives do we want to lead? Above all, will we forever enjoy
being tyrannized by things?

Many of the answers, in terms of rich living, depend
on the uses we make of this boon of fission. Of course,
our homes and factories will use increasing power. In
1924 we used only 455 kilowatt-hours per person. By
1950 this became 2,888. To use this we produced over
40 per cent of the electric power of the world. Russia,
with more people, was a poor second, producing only
one fifth as much as we did.

The demand for electricity has doubled in our land
every ten or twelve years since industry began. By 1976
our generating capacity will be eight or ten times as great
as in 1950. Farms will more than double their needs by
1960 and quadruple them by 1976. Industrial uses will
treble by 1976. But the home is the yearning mouth. A
completely electrified home could use over 25,000 kilowatt-hours per year to run future types of electrical
equipment.

But cheaper energy is not the sole fairy of the future.
A twin appears in our midst. Electronics comes to reduce
the drains on human energy expenditures. There will be
no fog-bound ships or planes; radar will become a traveler's TV; trucks may be propelled on special highways
without drivers, following the pattern of directed missiles,

electronic road warnings; electronic business machines will mathematize our affairs, and so forth. One electronic stock machine today tabulates daily inventories of a quarter of a million different items. No baseball games called off on account of rain, air fields always free of snow. With the aid of electronics we will be able to make one pound of Uranium 235 equal to three million pounds of coal.

No docks or railroad sidings will be needed for fuel, no storage dumps in sight. Smokestacks will disappear, as will telephones poles. Efficient reactors could cut the cost in 1976 to at least an equivalent of two dollars a ton for coal. Moreover, there will be no geographic limitations for location of our industries since the new energy is mobile. New industrial processes will flow from isotypes and superhot furnaces. Nuclear district steam heating will be usable in areas having a population density of 13,000 per square mile, which will take in those cities that now use over 10 per cent of our national comfort heating load.

When we once get going, we will reach an average construction rate for reactor capacity of about 25 million kilowatt-hours per year. Many experts, however, believe that since much of our power needs will be in small units —cars, ships and homes—a high per cent of the total energy may well come from solar rather than atomic energy. In any event, our biggest dollar export will consist of all kinds of new power generators. We use over three metric tons of coal per head, England over four, and India under one tenth of a ton. Italy is starting to employ volcanic power, and New Zealand has harnessed some geysers. To all the less developed countries we will gradually sell power. Gradually, of course, is the mood, since power without outlets and fixtures is a meaningless toy.

This revolution of power should confound no one who lived before 1900. My father came over as an immigrant in a sailboat from Europe; he drove a surrey to work in New York City; Welsbach lights were the caution area of my childhood home; we cooked by coal and wood; and my family was afraid of the speed of the Twentieth Century train to Chicago. No factory used a belt. If you are loath to use your hopes, just pause and consider the changes in your own lifetime, changes so gradual that their violence went unnoticed. It is both good and bad that man takes mutation in casual mood.

But all this new wealth is going to be subjected to great acceleration because of research to an extent unimaginable in 1920. At that date only 300 companies had laboratories, and employed only 9,300 people. By 1941, 2,300 companies employed over 70,000 researchers at a cost of 300 million dollars. By 1976 this will grow into billions. Our colleges, the nesting place of dreamers, spent over 350 million dollars on research in 1952, which was 1,500 per cent more than they spent in 1940. In brief, the index of physical progress will be measured in the number and types of these brains. Energy units will be the base of comparative standards of living instead of the old-fashioned notions of manpower and man hours, which will drop out of our economic literature.

One presidential economic advisor predicts that by

1960 our growth of productive output will reach 500 billion dollars. A mere extrapolation of this rate of growth to 1976 gives us 700 billions for 1976 at 1951 dollars.

But these are total national figures. To make them meaningful for humans, just note:

In 1849—per capita income was $320 in 1950 dollars. Actually it was only $107 per annum in the then buying values.

In 1929—it equalled $1,000 in 1950 dollars after taxes.

In 1951—$1,500 after taxes.

But average figures could be meaningless—like the average temperature of 100° in a hospital when you are suffering from 105°! Fortunately the increased income that comes from energy and brains is constantly being spread with greater benefits to *more* people.

In 1913, 57 per cent of income receipts came from wages and salaries; today it is 71 per cent. Entrepreneur income fell from 27 per cent to 20 per cent; income from dividends declined from 6.4 per cent to 3.6 per cent; interest from 4.4 per cent to 2.4 per cent; and rents from 5.2 per cent to 2.4 per cent. The per cent of total income received by the lowest two fifths of our people increased 160 per cent between 1935 and 1948, while that of the top two fifths income receivers increased only 112 per cent. The top one per cent took home 14 per cent in 1930 but only 8 per cent in 1950.

In 1939 only 2.3 per cent earned over $5,000. In 1950 this figure reached 18.9 per cent. Our inheritance tax laws based on philosophies not likely to be easily revised will further reduce the gaps between extremes.

We now are a middle-class people, or in other terms, a wealthy proletariat. In 1939 only 7 per cent earned from $3,000 to $5,000; by 1950 this bracket applied to 35 per cent of our people. Median income in 1939 was $1,200; in 1950, $3,200. This wiser spread occurred while men worked fewer hours.

Personal consumption, which accounted for 230 billion dollars in 1952, will exceed 310 billion dollars by 1960 and account for more than 70 per cent of the total product by 1976. In other words, as our production plants are converted to use more and cheaper energies, we will not have to tighten our belts to put more of the national income into capital-plant expenditures. This single factor is one of the keys to our conflict with the dictators. Dictators can force down the living standards of their people for decades in order to build dams and factories for the future. In a democracy no elected official can perpetrate such a squeeze even though it might, perchance, pay off in future generations.

But we are only at the entrance of the exploration of our world's resources. Always remember that bauxite was once considered a valueless clay, and that we will soon need 400 per cent more than is seemingly available. Nickel and cobalt were at one time the names of evil mountain spirits and potassium salt fields were called *Abraumsalze*, meaning "to be discarded."

Fluorine alone used in fluorocarbons will replace organic compounds. Fluorocarbon tires will not oxidize, and unlike cloth fibers or plastics, will not burn or rust. The "waste" that industry now throws away will be found to have valuable residues. The chromium discarded by our tanning and dyeing industry can be used for valuable bichromates. Your motion picture film now holds a quantity of silver which can be salvaged after the film is no longer displayed.

Presently, it takes a United States worker one day and two hours to make a radio; in Russia it takes twenty-seven days. Electronics will give us even more radios with still fewer hours. The electronic industry, now so soon after its birth, has grown to a five-billion-dollar business. Its mechanistic contributions will monitor, load, remove, warn, and correct trouble. Machines will replace the man who watches the machine. An electronic brain will check its own health. Moreover an entire new profession is appearing: those who specialize in compacting and reducing. After any machine is made there are experts who can reduce its size and use of materials. In olden times detailed experimenting was regarded as a manual chore for slaves. The philosophers played with theories. Greek geometry was like a crossword puzzle. It was thus that Democritus conceived the atomic theory in 400 B.C. Once more the contemplators will come into their own. Our dreamers and planners will make work for machines and not for men and women.

Chapter 4

OUR POPULATION

THE GREAT IMPONDERABLE X OF ANY ESTIMATE OF OUR WAY of life in 1976 is not so much the total income, but rather how many of us there will be. On this subject a great new science has developed; and between population experts of good will the estimates vary as widely as do conjectures as to numbers of birds, trees, quadrupeds or even the national income. We now recognize that a prognosis of what man does to nature is capable of greater accuracy than what man does to man. The imponderable is of course the unfathomable changing desire of man rather than the increasingly detectable force of nature. Man's control of exterior natural forces appears to be simpler than man's control of himself or his influence on his fellow men.

Counting of heads is a fairly modern phenomenon. From Biblical times, during the Kingdom of David, up to the eighteenth-century debates in the British House of

Commons, a census was feared and avoided as a threat to liberty. Present-day guessers estimate that the world population two thousand years ago was around 250 million. It is difficult to give much credence to any retrospective guess when one learns, for example, that in 2000 B.C. Ur was supposed to have a population of 500,000 while now it has only 85,000. But the experts are not daunted. They estimate that it took seven hundred more years with ups and downs for the world population to reach a solid 300 million. Almost three thousand years later in 1650 the figure is supposed to have almost doubled to 545 million. Thereafter the increase became rapid. In 1850 the best-informed guess was 1¼ billion. By 1950 this figure had more than doubled.

The geometric growth of world population to the present 2½ billion in 1950 is fantastic in the light of war, famine, plague, infanticide, and the known decline in population curves after the introduction of modern industrialization. Agricultural China alone is supposed to have grown from 60 to 463 million in the 1,955 years of the Christian Era. The more medicine develops, the greater the danger of overpopulation.

The population estimates for 1976 for our nation range from 165 million to 225 million. For the year 1975, the President's Water Resources Policy Commission guessed 190 million, the President's Material Policy Commission came up with a figure of 193 million, and the figure of the Joint Committee on the Economic Report comes to

190 million for 1965. All these estimates are based on what is happening now.

We are growing at the rate of one person every thirteen seconds, three hundred an hour, or two million a year. *The monthly* average increase last year represents a city of about the size of New Haven, Connecticut; Salt Lake City, Utah; or Spokane, Washington.

Our growth in the past was much influenced by immigration. From 1780 to 1920 our population grew 40 per cent from natural increase of our original immigrant stock and 60 per cent from new immigration—an enriching flow of men and women of courage and strong work habits, people infected with the dream of freedom. This new population aided our culture and our economy even though we failed to see in it a vast westward migration, and hence bottled it up on the Eastern seaboard (save only for the Scandinavian influx in the Midwest).

The cruelty of the early comers toward the newcomers reached a peak when Irish men and women were stoned in the streets of New York, with an intolerance scarcely equaled since the burning of Quaker or Mormon buildings. Our commendable melting-pot theory was often given mere lip service, or on the other hand, was distorted to the point where the children of the more recent immigrants grew up ashamed of their unAmericanized parents and failed to appreciate their own great parental folkways. This led to deep rifts in immigrant homes and lost for all of us the richness of foreign mores.

From now on immigration will play a smallish role. With our exceptional high standard of living we think we are no longer able to let down the bars. From Russia alone, if we did, we would get millions who seek freedom, and from the free nations we would get those who look for better living standards. This is not to say that we could not enrich ourselves by doubling the figure of net immigration of about 200,000 a year. But at this moment of our history the labor-union fear of a glutted labor market is more determinative of our national policy than the remnant of employer desire to depress labor by creating an excessive labor reserve. Add to this the prevalent anti-alien attitude which cuts across many groups, and we find a reversal of our historic position of political and economic asylum.

Thus we muddle along, with hypocrisy administering the immigration relief program, while a neurotic fear of communist infiltration closes our ports to much needed skilled workmen, teachers and scientists. This, while three thousand miles of northern border are virtually unpoliced against dangerous revolutionists. In fact, any communist saboteur can come to our land without even wetting his feet in the Rio Grande.

Long before 1976, despite the reduction of hours of labor, we will invite to our shores thousands of researchers, inventors, teachers and workers in the arts and professions. In fact, a new competition between nations for such men and women of gifted mind will become active. These minds will represent the wealth of a nation. Already we hunt abroad for chemists and physicists who have dreamed further or differently than we have. By 1976 we will fully appreciate that our prosperity and peace of mind depend on the well-being of all other peoples, and the increased free transit of brains throughout the world will appear as a concomitant to the present flow of students, workers and vacation travelers.

Our present fearsome insistence on visas and other documents permitting entrance or exit will have disappeared. Before World War I passports were not in vogue, and in fact were used only for those who had fled military compulsions of another nation. In 1976 people will recapture their olden right to visit at will all parts of their earth. The present increasing number of visaless nations of Europe will soon enhance our shame and reduce our invalid fears. Joint passports, approaching a single United Nations Travel Document, will be accepted for all free peoples long before 1976. The recently enacted statute of *ne exeat*, "You may not leave," will be wiped off our law books by judicial opinion if not by legislative mandate.

Far more important than migration is the capacity and will of people to plan the size of the family. We are increasingly determining our own reproductive rate rather than continuing to let nature create excesses only to kill them off. Some nations practice compulsory price and wage controls to attain fuller employment. Most nations are aware of the vast wealth that flows from controls of animal propagation. But much of the planet still adheres to the luxury of sentimentality when it comes to human population controls. Hence, a low estimate for world population in the year 2000 is 3 billion.

It would be difficult to disagree with the anticipated horrors flowing from an overpopulated, underfed world were it not for one obvious boon for all mankind, close at hand. I refer, of course, to the contraceptive pill, or equivalent means of limiting the size of families to wanted children. I know of few population figures that have been predicated on the existence of a generally accepted esthetic, and effective, contraceptive. If the official figures of government agencies take new contraceptives into account, no special mention has been made thereof. The figure I arrive at is close to 190 million, but it assumes not only the new contraceptive but also the high prestige value of a family of two or three children—not one, nor more than three.

Although primitive man discovered and used contraceptives of a sort, little modern scientific research has gone into the varied possibilities of preventing ovulation without interference with menstruation. The four magic days when the ovum proceeds in the tube invite inquiry into the fluids which may relate to the flow. We are only now learning a little about the muscles which may affect the progress of the egg. There may even be an intrinsic mechanism, controllable like the beat of the heart. Studies of the bloodstream from the mother to the ovum and of the misplacement of the egg in the uterus, which often leads to involuntary abortion, may give us the solution to the overpopulation problem. Moreover, the male is not irrelevant

in this respect, and the solution might lie in the prevention of the generation of spermatozoa. In this direction,
there are experiments indicating a suspension of such generation with safety to the man's health for as much as three
months. The solution may come from the oil of the Calcutta
field pea now being investigated at Rochester, New York.

In brief, overpopulation is a greater cause of death,
disease and destruction of the family than any number of
diseases for which we presently spend millions. Cancer
and dystrophy elicit millions of dollars annually for research when in fact a smaller amount of money spent on
the prime disease of world overpopulation might bring better and healthier families, selected with freedom by
parents, with a reduction of unwanted children and result-
ant family tension.

The discovery of an effective inexpensive contraceptive faces a world population divided roughly into three
groups: one third under communist dictatorship; one third
living, generally speaking, under our democratic concepts;
and one third presently "uncommitted." The Communists,
opposed to contraception, exploit with great success the
difference in standards of living in the uncommitted third,
and it has been our special policy to win over the "uncommitted" by helping to raise their standards of living. But
living standards are not the result of production alone but
of production divided by population.

Some of our experts believe that the rest of the world
can never be supported at our standard of living. Such
authorities hold that increased production cannot keep

pace with an increase of thirty million population a year. There is much to support these gloomy prophets. However, we do know that the fertility-mortality relationship shifts in cultures in relation to the degree and types of industrialization. In our own society marriages decline in periods of depression and birth rates increase in times of prosperity.

We will easily adapt to this new contraceptive soon to be available in our land, while the cultures which need contraceptive advice far more than we do will have fewer people equipped to explain and handle the liberation of the new family. Generally speaking, we suffer from fewer restraining taboos, although we can learn from Nehru's leadership in India to accent the population aspects of living standards. Fortunately, the previous odd cultural accord between communist dictatorship and the Vatican is already being broken. The former will shift its position when it no longer burns to rule the earth, and when its serfs are allowed curiosity. The latter is already shifting as its parishioners feel a reduction in anti-Catholic attitudes and the sense of lessening need for greater Catholic populations.

A leading Catholic medical opinion supports the position that in five years, with five million dollars, the new contraceptive can be at hand. All we need in order to show up the fruitless race between food and people is to make available to all people the power and right to plan the size of their own families. In our Republic we will digest our odd mixture of ancient Greek and Jewish population attitudes. The Greeks, a people too numerous for their small area, limited their population by infanticide, homosexual practices and adultery; while the Jews, a small nation in a big land, adopted all the dogmas needed to multiply: approval of polygamy, condemnation of fornication, adultery and masturbation. We are fast learning that societal attitudes toward sexual and parental urges are not always remote from the fear of external enemies, or the adequacy of supply of soil, food or energy. In fact, as societies increase their standards of living, or envision the potentials of the leisure life, the parental urge operates toward that size of family which can be well supported and decently brought up to face its environment. The subjection of women—the ancient chattels of men—as mere breeding machines, gives way to the higher living standards produced only in a society of equality of sexes.

Attitudes toward extra-marital sexual outlets vary with cultures and population pressures. Parental urges are not to be completely isolated from sexual urges—not even by ill-fated attempts at total abstinence. In India, for example, the use of prostitution would relieve the starvation of unsupportable millions, but sexual monogamy contains prestige values sufficient to outweigh starvation or death. Mankind nowhere will leave female babies in the fields to die or permit millions of deaths at child birth. But by 1976 the great revolution produced by the new antifertility factor will save the human race from the hopeless search for enough sustenance to keep up with the millions of presently unwanted offspring. We will look back with incredulity on the practices of a minority of our population who deny themselves the joys of sexual marital outlets as a means of family limitation.

Our own population trends, though not unique, must be appraised vis-à-vis our culture. As distinguished from many other cultures, birth rates in our land show a wide fluctuation in the short term and a slow decline in the long term. The decline shows up in the lower frequency of fourth, fifth or more children in one family, while first and second births have shown no definite upward or downward trend. The birth rate for women aged forty-five to forty-nine is only one fifth as large as it was in 1921, while the rate for women aged fifteen to thirty has declined only one tenth in the same period. A more civilized attitude toward minorities has helped close the gap between the birth rates of native white, non-white and foreign born. The childbearing of Negro women has declined 50 per cent since 1850. Moreover, industrialization has naturally left impacts on population trends. In 1800, there were 1,352 children under five for every 1,000 women aged twenty to forty-four, varying from New England with 1,160, to the rural Northeast Central area with 1,900. In 1940 there were only 419 children under five per 1,000 women of that age group, varying from 269 in New York to 748 in the rural farm section of North Dakota.

Of course, the declining birth rate must be read against the decline in maternal and infant mortality. Maternal mortality declined from 6.47 per 1,000 live births in 1927 to 0.76 in 1951. In 1927, 65 out of every 1,000 babies born, died before they reached the age of one year. By 1951, this had declined to 29.

More spectacular than the birth-rate trends has been the decline in the mortality rate among younger age groups through medical science, as discussed elsewhere. As medicine conquers the principal killer diseases of today, and as the inequities between the white and non-white populations are removed, life expectancy will increase still further.

Declining immigration and birth rate, and increasing life expectancy, means an ageing of the population from a median of sixteen in 1800 to thirty in 1948 and possibly thirty-six in 1976. In 1840, 9 per cent of the population were forty-five to sixty-four years, today 20 per cent fall in that group, and by 1976 it will probably be more than a quarter of the total population.

There are now 12½ million people over sixty-five. By 1976 we will have millions over seventy-five. The working ages will change and the ratio of dependents to producers will not greatly increase and may decline, for most men will not want to retire at sixty-five. On the other hand, there will be a reduced proportion of producers because of the demand which modern technology will justly make for longer training periods before a worker can be productive.

The effect of an older population will soon call for a complete reappraisal of retirement attitudes. Retirement in present terms will not exist in 1976. The old folk will not be condemned to wasted, useless existences. Already we

see the shift in certain groups. A college professor's retirement age was sixty a decade or so ago; now it is sixty-five
or seventy. But the shift from teaching to retirement will
not imply a leap from work to loafing. Rather will the
amount of work—four courses to three, to two, to one—become the pattern of the future. Thus the physical and mental capacity to produce—lectures, soap or furniture—will
become the determinant of quantity of work, quantity of
leisure and quantity of compensation. The anomaly of our
present system is seen in retirement of professors at one
college only to be hired by another, while government employees retire with pensions to get other jobs.

The present fear that young couples will not be able to
carry on their backs the economic burden of supporting
the older folk creates no insurmountable problem. This is
particularly true because even now the old age pensions
program has its main benefit, not in providing for the
aged, but in releasing the energy of the young couples, re-
lieved from the necessity of providing direct support to indigent parents.

Another by-product of the age will be seen in the
construction of future homes, fitted for more families with
fewer children and fewer families with no children. Or-
phan asylums will be as outdated as debtors' prisons and
adoptions will be carried on with new attitudes which
will wipe out the punitive cruelties of present denomina-
tional segregation.

The population trend will produce a more homoge-
nous people. Due to immigration quotas, the proportions

of nationalities have remained substantially the same since 1920. In 1900, 13 per cent of us were foreign born, a figure reduced to 9 per cent in 1940 and 7 per cent in 1950. Moreover, in 1790, 80 per cent of the population was white; in 1940 this figure was 90 per cent. The number of "white" population was never subject to clear definition. Intermarriage is starting to legitimatize the interracial sexual relations which have produced our large mulatto population. The color of skin will no longer be, by 1976, a strong bar to social, sexual or marital boundaries.

In the meanwhile we will continue for some time to be taller and probably heavier. In World War II we found that our men were two thirds of an inch taller and one to ten pounds heavier than in World War I. And there is some evidence to indicate that the average girl entering college today is nearly one inch taller than the girl of a generation ago.

Our roaming population will not stay put. We all know of the great westward trek of our ancestors. The location of the population in the past was related to the abuse of improperly used soil, the dream of distant easy riches, the invitations of cheap power and cheap labor, and above all, the attractions of climate. Up to 1850 half of the people born in South Carolina moved out of the state. From 1850 to 1940 the Northeastern states attracted almost as many people as they lost. The West Central lost to the far West. From 1940 to 1950 California increased 50 per cent, Oregon 40 per cent and Washington 37 per cent. The South Atlantic states which lost population from 1870 to 1930 have been gaining proportionately since. The center of population in 1900 was Columbus, Indiana; in 1940 it was 110 miles westward in Sullivan County, Indiana; in 1950 it was 54 miles further west in Richland County, Illinois.

Further movements of our people will be prompted by a miscellany of causes. The impact of Pittsburgh-Plus (a billing device to favor Pittsburgh) and the location of railroad and airline stockholder controls in the East will no longer be such dominant factors. The removal from big cities to suburbs will be less significant than the flow to newly created centers of population. New cities are presently being built—for example, the steel mill town on the western side of the Delaware River at Trenton. Dozens of new cities will arise. The national flexibility of minimum-wage rates, the efficiency of city management reflected in tax rates, the proximity to market places and above all the profound pressure of working people and executives toward leisure living will replace the existing artificial or outdated urges for location of factories, mills and people.

The 190 million population of 1976 will increase our households from 43 million in 1950 to around 55 million in 1976, and our families from 39 million in 1950 to about 50 million in 1976. A household for this purpose means the entire group of persons who occupy a house, apartment or room that constitutes a dwelling unit. Thus a household, in times of depression, often contains more than one family. By 1976 a family will be a household even though not every household will contain a family. There will still be people living alone.

Control of population by man's own desires will create a social revolution that will markedly reduce the burdens of delinquency, ill health and antisocial attitudes which result from a family larger than the economic, physical and spiritual capacity of the parents. In that revolution, sex laws, concepts of illegitimacy and miscegenation will be revised. We will build our own environmental selective eugenics.

Population in one sense is numbers. But in its real meaning it is far more. It is men and women and children living in relation to each other and to the supply of goods; with an insight which makes that relationship unhurtful to others and leaves the individual always excited about a changing world. Such a population we will have in 1976.

Chapter 5

FOOD AND FARM

IF A FARMER IN ONE OF OUR COLONIES OF 1787 TOOK A TRIP abroad in 1955 to any of the countries of the East or Near East he would feel quite at home. Today the art of extracting food from the soil, for most of our planet, is identic with our own farm life of 1787. In fact, between 300 B.C. and about 1800 A.D. only three important advances were made in agricultural methods—the horse-collar, the scythe and the cradle used with the scythe.

Now at last we are approaching in agriculture a change as dramatic as the shift from water power to atomic fission in the industries of our Republic.

At the time our nation was founded, the American farmer could provide only for his own family and for about one sixth of another person. More than 90 per cent of our people were agrarian. By 1870 our labor force was equally divided between farm and factory, which is approximately the present total world proportion. Today fewer than 15 per cent of us are farmers. If we had not improved our technology we would have starved, despite our great Western lands. Since 1930, while our population increased only 20 per cent, our food production climbed by more than 50 per cent. We consume per capita 1,600 pounds of food a year, on which we spend about one quarter of our family budgets, although its production occupies only about nine million people.

In 1850, power per farm was 1.8 horsepower, and it literally came from a horse or other animal. By 1930 each farm was using about 12½ horsepower and all but 1¼ was mechanical. By 1950 the total grew to 33 horsepower and less than one horsepower came from animals. Over those twenty years the *output* per man hour on the farm, on an index of 100, grew from 87 to 164.

No economic change in our Republic is as fascinating as our dramatic somersault from agriculture to industry. The first report of our Secretary of the Treasury—The Report on Manufactures (1791)—shows great concern for the proper relation between agriculture and industry. Industrial income and prospects for manufacturing were certainly negligible. Hence a recommendation was made to subsidize American industry by the use of tariffs. The argument was simple. If we protect the American manufacturer, he will make more money and he and his employees will buy more farm products and enrich the farmer. During the last few decades this thesis has been preached in reverse: We must protect farm incomes by subsidies and then the farmers will buy more of the city-folk production, and this will aid the industrial areas. Thus both Alexander Hamilton (1791) and Henry A. Wallace (1940) point to the constant need of equilibrium and the mutual interdependence between the two great sectors of our economy. The only difference is that the underdog shifted.

City folk are inclined to believe that the farmer's problems are solved when they read of encouraging progress, such as that 62 per cent of farms were self-owned in 1920, and 74 per cent in 1950, or that farms with electricity grew from one million in 1930 to five million in 1950. But farmers no longer live isolated lives and their desires must be viewed comparatively as well as objectively. They can now more easily compare their lot with that of city people, and their desires have grown more rapidly than the improvement of their condition.

Indeed, the economic and social history of our nation might be told in terms of the changing relationship between industry and agriculture, or city and country folk. Despite improvements in income of those who grow our food, the improvement is not comparable to that of factory workers. We are as yet far from equalization of prosperity Agriculture gets only 6 per cent of the national income but contributes about 15 per cent of our workers; and although commerce and manufacturing receive profit comparable to proportionate use of labor, finance captures 9 per cent of our income with only 3 per cent of our labor.

The subsidies paid to farmers are less than half the

amount paid to businessmen, even excluding the tariff.
In 1953, business received over one and a quarter billion
from our Treasury. To organize political lobby power for
millions of scattered farmers is about as difficult as finding
a qualified spokesman for small retailers or fishermen.
That the average distance of farm from trading center is
only six miles, whereas at the turn of the century it used
to be over thirty miles, only educates farmers to the disparity in treatment. The automobile, radio and television
likewise induce the farmer to make living-standard com-
parisons.

For many decades business has been nursed, subsidized and tariff-protected. The Reconstruction Finance
Corporation, in two decades of existence, made over
240,000 loans of more than 13 billion dollars to business
—and most of it to big business. By and large the farmers
were left to scrape for themselves, entering one by one
(a few by cooperatives) into the only market place in our
land that still maintains many of the attributes of free
trade in an economy controlled by accords and agreements
among producers and middlemen. The farmer, groping
for himself and without mechanization, as a lone operator,
brought his production to market and sold it then and
there. He had no choice of refusal, withholding or com-
bining with other sellers. Antitrust laws were not inspired
by agricultural production agreements in restraint of trade
and were seldom invoked against buyers who corrupted
the market place of the farmer.

Until recently we met the food demands of our in-

creasing population by opening new crop areas through
irrigation and land clearing. However, during the past
fifteen years we obtained only 38 million acres through
these methods. Still, in that period, we added the equivalent of 64 million additional acres by science and technology. This, even though in the past fifty-five years our
federal government spent less on farm research than it
spent in one non-war year—1951—on the military. In 1951
the federal and state governments spent only 60 million
dollars on agricultural research.

By 1976, with an improved diet and 190,000,000 people, we will need 627 million acres of crop land or its
equivalent. We now have 462 million. A small part of
the difference will come from 15 million acres released
from feeding horses and mules, and twice as much by
irrigation, drainage, flood control et cetera. That will
leave the equivalent of 120 million acres to come from
science—not counting the decreasing fertility of the soil
at the rate of about seven tenths of one per cent a year.

In the rest of the world the race between food and
population presents even more disturbing problems. We
have a caloric intake of about 3,000 a day. Much of the
Orient is below 2,000. Yet if all the earth's land could
be employed as the best now is, the planet could support
ten times its present population. But soil is the child of
weather. Our hope lies in the fact that we are beginning
to dominate weather. In Eastern Tennessee we stripped
the land for copper; temperature increased three degrees,
wind velocity climbed, evaporation doubled and precip-

itation declined 20 per cent. Eastern United States temperature increased 2 per cent since 1875. The North
Pole moves enough each year to chart its migration, the
ice front on the Alaskan Bay retreated sixty miles in 140
years, the corn line has traveled northward five hundred
miles in the past twenty years, the green crab migrates
north and kills the steamer clams, sardines shift from
California to Spain, our mean temperature has increased
4 per cent in a century, the Iowa growing season is twenty
days longer than in 1910, and the polar caps recede five
hundred feet a year!!

These few odd samples present but a small part of
man's knowledge about climatic changes and soil fertility.
Even individual farmers, who at times possess occult
weather senses, are seldom likely to view weather except
by the day, month or crop season. If I understand correctly
Joseph's prophetic dreams of cyclical changes, man has
possessed much unused knowledge for thousands of years.
Only now are we about to apply our knowledge, not just
for prophecy, but for creating conditions which will make
us win the race between food supply and population.
Man will master weather. Weather will be his servant.
We will not only predict the tornado but prick it to death.
We will place rain where we want it and move it from
acres and peoples where it is unwelcome. The rain-making
business, presently profitable, will be deemed a public
function by 1976, controlled by the federal government.
Cities and states were not bounded to cope with rain. It
is not enough to invite or push along the life-giving water

for one small area, unconcerned with what this means to its neighbor. We will create weather with discrimination. I should think that the most rewarding financial investment of our government in a decade or so will be the manufacture of climate. Russia already spends great fortunes on this aspect of its food supply.

Predictions for farmer and fisherman will no longer fall in the realm of prophecy, but will more closely resemble railroad timetables. The democratic resolution of where to spill the heavenly water and where to hold it back will require regional and interstate play of forces exerted on our nationwide government. It will take great wisdom to rain on Peter and to let Paul go dry. The head of the Weather Bureau will be one of the top men in our secondary cabinet and probably as important as the future Secretary of Agriculture. The causation, selection and cost of weather-making will naturally be related to timbering, smoke dispersal, fog piercing and iceberg controls.

For ages, man has been more concerned with fighting cold than heat. Chimneys preceded by thousands of years the first air conditioner, installed, interestingly enough, in the House of Parliament in 1836. Air conditioning is a modern concept, not necessarily a luxury in relation to the use of man's energy and production. The climate-makers of the future will be able to provide us with both desired heat and desired coolth.

The contribution to our food production by these new techniques of rain- and weather-making will of course be

on a magnificent scale. But the collateral effects will also
carry great import. We will say "Halt" to the Torrid
Zone in its northward march. Weed killers will be usable
in a climate-controlled tropical equatorial zone, and arable
land will become available in the now Frozen North. The
blue-winged warblers will be stopped in their flight northward, and the turkey vulture may even return to the
South. Man will be healthier, since the body is at its best
when its waste heat is dissipated as soon as possible; and
he will produce more wealth.

But this is only a start of the new revolution in food.
The supply of ocean water is about to be tapped. It is
anyone's guess whether fresh water will be derived from
salt water by treating brackish sources, by distillation or
by freezing methods. I doubt, however, if the present
proposals of floating icebergs from the Arctic to the California Coast will be needed. The State of Kuwait on the
Persian Gulf has already placed an order for a distillation
plant producing a million gallons of good fresh water per
day. Solar distillation may become the answer. Possibly a
tray area of a couple of hundred thousand acres will do
the trick more cheaply. Vast stretches of our seaboards
may be flooded for the development of sea food, with the
building of fish farms. We will be able to accelerate the
propagation rate of fish on inland farms.

Beyond such advances surely to be attained by 1976,
we will convert the slogan of "Swords into plowshares" to
"Plowshares into chemicals." The chemist and the weath-

erman will be even more important than the hero Patrick
Henry had in mind when he said "the greatest patriot is
the man who stops the most gullies."

We are starting to look inside food, and the knowledge of its composition spells wealth. One item alone—
corn hybridization—brought us a present advantage of
three billion dollars a year. Fertilizers for plants have
been reconstituted so as to give nutriments in one, instead
of innumerable, doses. We now spend one billion a year
on fertilizers, but new chemicals will act more directly,
effectively and cheaply. Our present loss of four billion
a year (nearly half of our total education bill) from fungi
and plant diseases will be cut in half, and our weed bill
of five billion a year will be down to the vanishing point.
Already we have found herbicides that kill only the broad-
leaved plants and leave the grasses unharmed. Undesirable
growth—if in our new chemical age it is allowed to any
extent—will be cheaply exterminated. Insecticides are
the play toys of today. Soon we will say "finis" to the
boll weevil by using a poison to be absorbed, not sprayed.
Any spraying that will continue until 1976 will be done
from the sky from our new slow-flying planes. In 1955 it
takes five workers sixty hours to weed-control one hundred
acres; but by air, in thirty minutes one pilot and four
workers can do the same chore.

Growth regulators will control the rate and type of
development of vegetable and animal. Fodder crops will
be produced from plants, unusable today because they
contain toxic constituents. Untold is the magic of farm

chemistry. Tomatoes become seedless by use of indole-
butyric acid on their unfertilized ovaries; apples and pears
will grow, if we want them, to the size of grapefruit.
Prevention of premature blossoming or shedding will reg-
ularize the farmer's life.

Chemistry will produce three-pound broilers in nine
weeks instead of eleven; two thousand pounds of beef in
the time it now takes to build up six hundred pounds;
sows will be bred three times a year instead of twice and
will bear twice the number of baby pigs as there are
nipples. By artificial insemination a bull will serve two
thousand cows a year, instead of forty or fifty. Our new
seeds will have built-in enemy destroyers—herbicides, fun-
gicides and even colors which will repel or invite birds
and insects. Beyond these prognosticated events, we will
approach soilless agriculture. Chemically enriched water
is already commercially used for growing tomatoes, beans
and cucumbers.

Algae farming is opening up—fifty thousand pounds
of protein to the acre—grown even on decomposing sew-
age, thus reducing the needs of disposal. We have located a
single-celled alga known as chlorella. This is nothing new.
It was always in existence close to man. The only thing
new is our power of discernment of its sources and detection of its qualities, chief of which is that it is over 50
per cent protein. Its suitability for chicken feed is already
proven at fifteen dry tons per acre. It has peculiar possibilities for human food consumption, particularly because
the yield per acre is fabulous, and it possesses convert-

ibility into foods of many flavors and textures. Clothing may even be made out of some algae. A crew of a few score of men will be able to handle the entire operation of a ten-thousand-acre algae farm. Fifty million acres of such farming could virtually feed the world, and poor soil is no detriment to its rapid growth.

But maybe the greatest increase of food will come from the ocean. The quantity of plants produced in the seas by photosynthesis is ten times the amount produced on land. Plankton, that microscopic food loved by whales, may be the vogue for humans by 1976. Fish farmers with freezing and shipping facilities will help fight the population problem.

In the past, when so-called "cheap" supplies were cut off, man's ingenuity discovered more abundant and equally economic sources of the materials he needed. Beet sugar was discovered during the Napoleonic Wars when the continent was blockaded. The Germans discovered a way to make sulphur from cheap calcium sulfate when cut off from usual sources during the war. The Haber process for making nitrates made us independent of our former Chilean source during World War II. During the Japanese occupation of the South Pacific area, we developed synthetic rubber. Today 65 per cent of all rubber used in the United States is synthetic. Its tread-wear performance is 20-40 per cent better and its price is 20 per cent lower than the natural. It is made from low-cost petroleum hydrocarbons. Today 99 per cent of our dyes, 75 per cent of our drugs and medicinals, 20 per cent of textiles are synthetic. Natural gums and resins account for only 5 per cent of the 2.3 billion pounds of plastics.

In the battle over synthetic foods of the next decades I take a position on the side of the imitators of nature. It is high time we freed mankind from its bondage to the plant. Synthetic dyes freed 350,000 acres of land in Europe (madder-red) and one and one-half million acres in India (indigo blue). Synthetic perfumes, jewels and other desiderata of our subtler senses have replaced nature's original products. In synthetics we will not consume the poisons found in natural foods—"avidan" in raw egg white, "dopa" in beans, et cetera. Texture and smell—basic elements of taste—can be synthetically produced. We will eliminate obnoxious odors—thus making available raw materials now too odorous for use. We know what gives raspberries, meat, et cetera, their distinctive flavors. We will re-create all edibles, as we have with cinnamon. From the air we will get carbon dioxides to be converted into the starch equivalents of wheat, corn and rye. Fats and oils will flow from glycerol factories. There will be no planting in the future for materials for clothing. Synthetics will take the place of cotton, silk and wool. Electronics will control the course of tractors so that no driver will be needed. If you doubt it, buy yourself a lawn mower controlled from your front porch, or a model airplane whose flight is controlled from the ground at a distance of a mile or more.

The thirty million more mouths to be fed—not to

mention empty stomachs abroad—will be supplied by science.

With our vast capital, and the leisure necessary for invention, we will be called on to help feed those portions of the world that are short of food—but not for long. Soon the secrets of uncostly growth will be exportable and easily usable. Then, as with all other export trade, indigenous expansion of local soil production will reduce the needs for outside help. Thus will the world become healthy, wealthy and possibly wise, provided only that family limitation, as elsewhere indicated, is no longer restricted by law, dogma or social taboos. Food will then keep up with the race of population.

Already in our partial leisure world about one sixth of all our home-eaten vegetables are home grown. With our new leisure and the new chemistry of 1976, the home (in the decent-sized community) will be a miniature chemical vegetable farm. Then mass experimentation will begin and poets of the soil will lead our people. The challenge to improve standards will be met with increasing health for all our people; greater variety of color, smell, taste and texture in our foods, and a not-to-be-underestimated growth in the factory food business. In fact, of all the sectors of our economy, agriculture will show the most dramatic advances. The progress will be refined, in the true sense of that word, since these are the people who are close to nature. They will no longer be glorified in terms of sweat and long hours, but for more valid reasons, because whenever man learns to battle—or cooperate—with nature he is playing with the infinite.

The personality of the American farmer is the keystone of our Republic. He represents the man or woman who cannot be seduced from the soil. Of those who left for the tinsel of the great illusory White Way, many returned. These peculiarly represent the vital strength of our economic life in that they tried out the two worlds and made their reasoned choice. In 1976 the farmer will be of that group which finds joy in his daily occupation. Outside outlets to satisfy creativity are less needed by those who watch things grow.

Research for the farmer will be no novelty. It will merely change its base. Mechanical and electrical equipment (we have four million tractors on our farms) has already created a great mass of scientific skills in our agrarian culture, but chemistry will be the revolutionary agent of farm and food.

The leisure of the farmer may for a time find outlet in the diverse avenues employed by the city folk who are unable to amuse themselves, and must be entertained by others. But the farmers of 1976 will need an escape to passive leisure as little as do biochemists or mechanical engineers. I suspect that the proportion of mental instability in farmers, compared to present city factory workers, is far less, and that the higher city figures will by 1976 be reduced to the farmer record. In the near future the pressure for better, more and longer education will be led by the farmers of the nation. Even today farm adult education demands exceed all others with nearly a million students at our agricultural colleges.

Rapidly a trend will arise to give the farmer of the future the standard of living, the cultural facilities and the prestige which he deserves.

Chapter 6

MARKET PLACE OF BUSINESS

THERE IS NOTHING INEVITABLE ABOUT THE GOOD DAYS TO
come to our people by 1976. Vision and direction by
human minds must still be applied to the happy use of
fission and electronics, and the satisfying employments of
our new leisure.

I believe that our nation faces a dire paradox in the
field of industrial enterprise. I refer to the loud shouts in
favor of free competitive enterprise that come from those
very persons who are destroying competition and driving
us toward government supervision, regulation and ultimate ownership. I would be less than frank if I did not
state the high values I place on competition, the fears I
have of excessive power and the certainty that a too-big
State spells loss of human individuality. In brief, I hold
that criticism is the essential and prime corrective in life
for individuals, businesses and governments. Since few

people are secure enough to welcome adverse criticism, critics are suppressed with dispatch if the power of suppression resides in the criticized. Only the secure can freely admit error. As a corollary, power is the main corrupter in life, particularly such kind and degree of power as can throttle criticism. Ten or twenty million dollars invested in real estate in New York or Chicago is relatively powerless and impotent, while the same sum might control and even wipe out all competitive correctives in paper-bag fabricating, area grocery outlets, or flower-seed production. We have seen in our great but brief history that whenever an industry approaches single ownership or even develops a substantial reduction in competition, many urge regulation which leads eventually to operation by government.

The danger that faces us in the further concentration of business into so few units as to imply absence of essential competition, is the take-over by the government; the government in turn waxing so big as to be highly inefficient, and trying to free itself from adverse criticism by the use of its claimed censorship powers.

The corrective weapon of voting is scarcely an adequate answer to this type of danger. In the first place, our national elections represent an endeavor to discover the mind of millions of widely spread and uncommunicative citizens. Moreover, at each national election innumerable issues of importance to different groups or sections of our people are up for consideration at one time. Subsidies for farmers, income-tax rates, attitudes toward defense planning and every conceivable issue has to be balanced one by one against a party or candidate's program on monopoly of the market place. On a referendum I have no doubt where our people would stand, but in a melee of issues bigness is probably the most difficult of all to define into voting dimensions. In fact, the objective tests of bigness must always relate to considerations of each commodity, and above all to man's increasing capacity to delegate authority.

In 1904 the so-called trusts already had in their hands 40 per cent of all our manufacturing capital. Thirty important products had been brought under virtual monopoly control, and twenty-six companies controlled 80 per cent or more of production in their fields. Self-employed people accounted for 37 per cent of the gainfully employed in 1880; by 1940 they accounted for fewer than 20 per cent, and now we find the figure to be only 17 per cent.

In 1909 the two hundred largest nonfinancial corporations owned 33 per cent of all assets of all the nonfinancial companies in our land. In 1929 they owned 48 per cent, and now own over 60 per cent. The four biggest companies in their fields now control 55 per cent of motor-vehicle production, 67 per cent of blast furnaces, 76 per cent of tires, and 90 per cent of cigarettes. And so we go down the path of diminishing competition in business after business. Our antitrust laws have not stemmed the

tide. Fission and electronics will further favor private concentration, to be followed by government ownership and
operation.

In front of our eyes we see the evaporation of competition. During the last war the Pentagon, understandably,
placed its biggest orders with the biggest companies.
Thus, it aided the drive toward a monopoly market by
lazily permitting prime contractors to select and hence
dominate secondary "bits and pieces" subcontractors, instead of selecting thousands of small companies for direct
relations with our government. Whenever a giant con-
tractor deals with hundreds of subcontractors a degree of
economic peonage ensues, for, as the "big boys" brag, they
can always pull the stopper and the subcontractor goes
down the drain. In my own lifetime I can recall the days
when the size of corporations was limited by state legislatures, and I have witnessed the corporate lobbies remove
all such size limitations. Fairly recently the scandals of
life insurance companies were investigated by a later
Chief Justice who led most of the companies into mutualization, thus still further removing the controls over management which reside in the veto power of stockholders.
Today insurance companies manage over eighty billions
of our assets, a growth of thirty-three billions since 1948.
In 1900, their assets were under two billion dollars.
Nearly one half of all this wealth is invested in private
industry and finance. About twenty-five billion is invested
in buildings. Thus, a few directors decide if your city is
to have a new skyscraper, apartment-house development

or industrial plant. No competition is left in the insurance business except at the level of the local agent, and he gets his business usually on friendship—certainly not because he is selling a better or cheaper policy. One insurance company (a mutual) has more than thirteen billion of assets to supervise, and has an annual income larger than the total budgets of twenty-two states added together. Such an economic empire is run by a small group of self-perpetuating trustees, hiding their power behind the impotent right of each policyholder to vote his policy in the election of trustees. This right is so unreal that it is never used, and the insurance trustees are fully appreciative of this fact. I am confident we will limit these mammoth piles of power to areas, and provide that no insurance company may operate outside of a single Federal Reserve District, of which our nation has twelve. That will be enough for any group of mortals to direct. To have a billion or two of assets to manage and to be responsible to no stockholders (as is the case with most of the companies since mutualization) leads to laxities so terrifying that even a recent exposé was played down to the point where the corrupt nepotism of a president brought the other directors neither to shame nor resignation. Without a revision of life-insurance-company power, freedom will be difficult to maintain.

As power fell into fewer and fewer hands, through government indifference or even affirmative assistance, the relation of government to industry carried far different implications than in our early days. In 1791, a group of

businessmen were taken by Alexander Hamilton to visit
Passaic Falls, New Jersey. There a site of 700 acres
was purchased for $8,230 to contain "American industry."
The company was to get tax exemption, and $160,000 was
paid into the company treasury to be spent for: a canal
$20,000, a weave shop $5,000, a cotton shop $5,000, print
works $10,000, and fifty houses for workers at $250 apiece.

But 1955—and even more so 1976—is a different
world than 1791. In a century and a half we traveled far
from home weaving, home shoemaking and Paul Revere's
silver shop. On coal, oil and water we built vast economic
empires, and as we built we contantly transferred from private to public hands those undertakings for which competition seemed at the moment to be wasteful or too expensive. Ironically, the leading exponents of freedom of
business from government interference often begged government to take over business, provided the profit of each
transition was inviting enough. When private financiers
guessed wrong on the profitability of the Cape Cod Canal,
they urged socialization of that waterway, but at a good
price.

Thus we have made important transfers from private
to government operation on seemingly unique and prag-
matic grounds, later justifying the expansion of the sovereign power by a variety of pleasing philosophies. Competition is too expensive. Service will be better. Above all,
the operation is affected with a public interest. To any and
all abstract philosophies used in the past we must now add
a consideration of the danger to freedom through busi-

ness or government growing too big. And even on that high level of debate men of good will, desirous of freedom, will urge that the line be so drawn that the new "energies" reside in government and not in private hands. To which it can be answered: If the government owns power, it owns all else, for what use is the freedom to use a skill or capital if the ultimate control resides at the power gate? This new Bigness-Freedom issue will have to be resolved in a different kind of debate from that which surrounded previous issues, which seem to some to be analogous. The danger does not lie in a word such as socialism, nor in the idea of community ownership. It derives only from the absence of competition—the removal of that corrective so badly needed by all men and institutions to keep man on his toes.

In 1787, fire companies were run for profit, at times under the slogan "No money, no squirty." Surely no one seriously suggests private fire-fighting, even though separate borough departments in big cities would result in great savings and improvements. Our mails were run for decades by private investors but finally, to avoid duplication and competition, the government was handed the monopoly. On the value of the absence of such competition there might be honorable disagreement. At least it can be said we have competition to the point where faster services still remain in private hands—telegrams, telephones, and express.

But the main shift from private to public control came in the utilities—gas, light, water—which we delusively described as "peculiarly affected with a public interest." Regulation or ownership of gas, light, water and transportation to varying degrees, enlarged the power of city, state and federal governments. Unlike many other free nations, we have not taken over into government ownership and operation the telephone, telegraph, railroads and airlines. I suspect the reason we have left a private grip on such enterprises is that we have believed that the present monopolistic loss of competition could be offset in part by government fixation of rates and profits. We imagined also that the worst of such frauds as inevitably follow absence of critical competition, would be caught by federal or state banking, insurance, utility or transportation commissions. We relied on objective wisdom of government commissions to arrive at fair rates and fair profits, a bit of statistical acrobatics which must always be attempted when competition vanishes.

But in each instance we further encourage the reduction of competition. Your insurance premium is the same no matter which company you deal with. Your state fixes noncompetitive premium rates. The choice of a savings bank in your town, or convenient to your home in a big city, is restricted by the state, which sees to it that only that number of banks is licensed as will leave profits satisfactory to the existing banks. The very act of licensing all new banks, et cetera, is a confession that these businesses cannot afford the luxury of full competition. Moreover, maximal interest rates on loans are fixed by penal laws, and you will never know how much the fixing of gas, light and telephone rates reduces the need for zeal, thrift and ingenuity on the part of the owners or managers of such enterprises. We spend twenty-nine billions for utilities, sixteen billion more than we spend on *all* the services rendered to us by the forty-eight states. Moreover, our utility companies, immune from competition, become increasingly less efficient, as would any humans whose only correctives come from random complaints by consumers or rulings by those government agencies which are set up to guarantee rates sufficient to bring reasonable dividends to owners. Since we debate only our political budgets, we have lost sight of many important comparatives in our utility budgets.

Oddly enough, most of our deviations from the competitive market have not occurred because of socialist or totalitarian ideology. Paradoxically we see the political party which presumably represents the biggest of businesses encouraging the growth of monopolies. For some odd reason it fails to recognize that, faced by monopolies, our public will eventually prefer the government-run monoploy to the state-supervised private monopoly. To my thesis that the tide of concentration must and can be stemmed, the cynic answers: "Since every small businessman is aiming to be a monopolist, you can't set back the tide. We are in for it! Bigger and ever bigger business! More and more government supervision to prevent the excesses of noncompetitive markets. And finally, after the breakdown of government supervision, government takeover of business may be the only move in sight." Just as some people want to brag that they will be the richest men in the graveyards, so also others seem to cherish personal profits more than the validity of their public declarations in favor of competition and "free enterprise."

There is much truth in this sad picture, for a too big government will produce failures which in time will result in a reduction of the rights of public criticism. Today it is not easy to get into the mass media any criticism of the telephone, light or gas companys, but imagine an election when the state *is* the utilities and the transportation system of our Republic. The present greater latitude of adverse comment on government rather than on big business can easily shift as soon as the government passes a point of societal equilibrium. Surely we must appreciate such difficulties of the democratic process in a country our size, compared to the Low Countries, Scandinavia or nations the size of one of our states, with populations less than that of one of our outrageously large cities.

As if we did not face enough difficulties, we now come to electronically usable fission—so different from any earlier problems. In the early 1800's our Congress voted three thousand dollars to help set up in business a glass blower in Pennsylvania. Governmental relationship to such early enterprises—or even to a waterfall or, later, to a coal mine—was quite different from governmental attitudes today toward the business of a fission, electronic, thermostatic industrial age. Leaving aside the military security aspects of fission, its conversion into peaceful power requires such capital as to leave the operation either to the government or, at best, to a few score gigantic private conglomerations of capital and know-how. Thus the new energy further pushes us into statism.

Possibly the very threat of statism through control of new energy sources will force us to answer the urgent appeals of minority voices to preserve free enterprise from overbigness in all other areas of the industrial market place. If we concede fission to the government, then to save ourselves from statism we will have to break up the over-big; prevent future concentrations of power; and preserve with strictness competition in all areas not necessarily assigned to government.

Vital forces with well-documented ideas have long presented a program to resist such statism in America. The dreams of the American business giant may now at last come up against still stronger dreams—the dreams of freedom. First and foremost in these forces is the American labor movement. Despite a smattering of socialistically inclined labor leaders, organized labor does not look with equanimity on the loss of freedom which inevitably follows when the government takes over a private business. Moreover, it is interesting to note that organized labor has usually urged government ownership only if private business has gone bankrupt, no longer faces competition or is unable to meet collateral competition, as for example, coal versus oil.

Various trends support my hopeful thesis in the battle against bigness and statism. Democracy within trade unions is fast growing; women are rising in labor leadership echelons; unions have responsibilities of vast treasuries, and are learning to manage what may be 100 billion dollars in health, welfare and pension funds, and with the heavy weight of inheritance taxes, stockholdings will be widely spread among all individual workers. With the shift from family or small group domination to widespread worker-owner participation, labor leadership with preferential balloting will soon be associated in the management of business. New techniques for expressing power will be developed as concentration of holdings disappear and masses of stockholders arise. In fact, labor is anticipating this next era of its activity. So long as management would not deal with organized labor, the unions were controlled by Communists, demagogues, or racketeers. Labor met capital's bigness by autocratic over-bigness of labor. Responsible leadership, however, quickly followed the employer's honorable recognition of the rights to organize. The Gompers'—shorter hours and more pay—craft movement was soon followed by the era of industrial unionization, and the wholesome though irritating competition known as jurisdictional disputes. Labor is already showing signs of an ability to help management reduce wastes of production and distribution. Who knows better how to do a job than the man who does it? With the education of our people this knowledge, presently often incommunicable, will be put to the greater service of our productive system. Above all this, we already see unions financing employers, as in the hat business; with management, conducting industrial surveys, as in the clothing industry; and jointly preparing profit-sharing plans, as in innumerable industries. The vast profit which ordinarily invites owners to merge with other plants, or sell out to the government, will be remote from the workers' dreams of better working conditions. They will still cherish the freedom of protest to management, and participation with management. The potential of low tax rates on the sale of a few shares of stock will not sway the working stockholders. Moreover, we will approach something like an annual guaranteed wage for workers along the lines of job security now provided for management—the over-riding inducement presently held out to workers by government operation. Then the government's advantage of lifetime jobs will no longer be of importance. Other visible trends against government operation are, on one hand, the fear of the loss of the freedom to strike; and on the other hand, fabulous plans such as the Sears, Roebuck one, which provide retirement conditions for a worker comparable to that of an upper-middle-class capitalist. A hundred and twenty thousand employees of that company own over 25 per cent of its stock. One particular worker who contributed a total of $3,762 to the Sears profit-sharing fund over a period of thirty-seven years, on retirement withdrew stock worth $118,250. The Sears plan, although unique in results if not in form, is still not generally accepted or understood. In any event, workers of the future will scrutinize profit potentials of prospective employers, and in so far as workers are invited to participate with their ingenuities, an interesting new type of competition between company benefit plans will come into being.

This system under which many companies have their workers as part owners will have to be given a new name. This new kind of profit sharing will avoid the meaningless, though well-intentioned, concepts of the past decades wherein profits so distributed were unrelated to worker effort, or if related, never explained to workers or shareholders other than in falsely noble, paternalistic terms used to reduce the guilt feelings of over-lucky owners. Two-way communication between management and workers will develop into a new art; and uniformity of union contracts on a national basis will no longer be needed when plants no longer run away from unionized to non-union areas of the nation. Above all, unions will preserve capital from its worst failures. I refer to the excessive dispersal of dividends, which often results in the absence of reserves later required to replace outdated machinery. Labor sitting on corporate management boards would have prevented the economic impotence of New England textile plants which closed up in part because they never replaced the old machines. Labor's concern for reserves will reduce much of our industrial waste.

On the affirmative side of increased productivity, we will recognize that the values of competition are so great that the government will act as a spear as well as a shield. We will proceed in all fields as we have in legislating the breakup of utility companies. No branch business will be allowed unless there be an affirmative showing of economic value to the consumer. Surely we are realizing the analogy between absentee ownership of a gas company, and that of a newspaper, radio, grocery, drugstore, and many other businesses. Furthermore, we have often declared by legal caveat: "Stick to your business, Mr. Railroad, you can't be Mr. Air Service or Mr. Coalman." Thus, the present hedging of a textile business owning a chewing-gum subsidiary, or an auto manufacturer making washing machines, will come to an end. The "loss leader" will be attacked. The profit on cars of Company X will no longer be usable to compete against the independent maker of iceboxes. Competition is prostituted by Company X losing on icebox production the moneys earned in automobiles. When the optimum point of efficiency is reached by a gargantuan company we will find that it usually uses power in the market place to beat down competition. Our largest companies of multiple products will "spin off" parts of products and assets into separate companies via nontaxable stock dividends.

Over the decades since we first adopted our antitrust laws, we have often come close to keeping the government out of business not by limiting the zeal or the ingenuity of big business, but by preventing the use of power instead of brains in the market. The Robinson-Patman and Tydings legislation were designed to prevent mere piles of dollars being employed to prevent new or smaller enterprises entering or surviving in the market. We must now willingly concede that, unrestrained by law, the greed of Big

Business will go beyond the point of optimum financial rewards to owners, or any direct relationship to reduction of consumer costs. Just as the government now says with general public approval that an agreement among competitors to fix prices or limit territory for trading is antisocial and illegal, so within a decade the science of statistical economics will lead us to predicate limitations on the size of businesses. The limits will be validly based on the visible lessening of profits after optimum size has been reached. There is no longer any doubt that U.S. Steel never made as good a return on capital or sales as did the moderate-sized steel companies. The savings banks of New York, as a previous study has proven, show reduced profits as soon as they top a quarter billion dollars of deposits of the public's nickels and dimes.

There are two bases for the argument against government ownership and operation of any business. First, the loss of ingenuity through the absence of competition, and secondly, decreases in returns—or, stated otherwise, increased costs—if the undertaking is too big. The same two factors apply also to business privately owned. In addition, I suggest that the corruption of big business goes way beyond the corruption of big government, whose officials when corrupted are corrupted inevitably and exclusively by business. If your mind goes to recent government scandals, I suggest that you inquire why the statistics of private bank embezzlements are no longer made public. The bigger the company, the more extensive and all pervading the corruption. It is only natural that whenever the markets are tight, the officials who have the power either to select potential customers or sources of supplies find themselves in the corruptive climate of free television sets, cars, or whatever will bring the needed results with some semblance of outward decency.

However, it is urged that research can only be carried on by Big Business. I call to your attention that the ten monopoly companies which owned nearly all of our anthracite coal saw no need for research nor for the use of their by-products, nor did they consider replanting the coal mountain tops with timber, to be needed sorely in future years for shoring up. Thus anthracite was unequipped to meet the competition of oil. The near monopoly of radio networks—there are fewer than ten, nation- and district-wide, in our land—is unable to meet the attack of television, though radio, if independently and competitively owned, would be able to do so.

Research theoretically should be peculiarly inviting to publishers, generally an informed group of people. And still whenever a newspaper in a city buys out or merges with its only remaining competitor, no research is undertaken to reduce rates to advertisers or price to readers.

Surely, in the future, our Bureau of Standards will offer special services for the researches of small companies carrying out tests which at present only the giants can afford. We make a sorry mistake if we forget the history of the great men of the past, men who stepped out of line

—a process less likely in the routinized big enterprises than in the shop of the sole operator or a small intimate partnership.

An inventor is a special kind of addict, and as monopoly affects a commodity, the inventor is sterilized because the monopolist does not have to research to build his markets, and the small competitor often does not dare fight the giant company. To big business, patents are often not instruments of reward to inventors, but weapons to be used against imaginative but less wealthy competitors. Since patents are in themselves monopoly grants from our government, I suggest that before 1976 there will be a split-up of the present patents into two kinds of protection. For the fundamental leaps of the brain, such as the invention of the vacuum tube, a long-term monopoly will be allowed. But for the bulk of patents, falling under the category of gadgets, no monopolies affording more than a two- or three-year head start will be granted. Moreover, all patents, particularly those dealing with First Amendment, health or security commodities, will be issued only on condition of compulsory licensing by the inventor of all companies which want to use the monopoly—of course at a fair royalty charged to the user and a decent profit to the inventor. Decisions along these lines are already flowing from our courts.

Another force contra the Bigness-to-Statism trend will follow the discovery of the waste of much of our present eight billion dollars of advertising. This advertising waste will no longer be encouraged by tax laws written for gargantuan business, under which the companies carry their advertising costs at only twenty cents on the dollar, with Uncle Sam paying at times the other eighty cents.

A revision of subsidies to business will be in aid of competition. The present business subsidies amounted to forty-five billion dollars over the past twenty years, or about forty-five times the subsidies to agriculture. A better market place will exist when commodities must find their own unsubsidized favor from the public. We have not revised our protective-tariff policy since 1930. The tariff subsidies to American business create not only artificial markets, but are costly to consumers. We will soon realize that we cannot sell abroad unless we will take payment in goods from the purchasing nations. We don't want their gold, and our consumers will benefit if we sell even to low-income people. Two obstacles to substantial tariff cuts across the board have been eliminated. First, organized labor has exploded the false myth that tariff cuts would create substantial unemployment. Second, excess production induces one industry after another to lobby for the right to receive from abroad payment in goods for our exported commodities. Of course we prefer to buy from low-cost nations and sell to high standard ones. Of course we prefer to sell commodities with large labor content and buy those with low labor content. But our plant is now so far in advance of that of most other nations that we will have little to fear in the way of competition even if we adopt free trade. By 1976 we will be a free trade nation—just as England was for more than a century during its greatest prosperity. In 1950 our international trade amounted to fifteen billions; by 1976 we will buy much more from outside our borders, but as production throughout the world shifts from man to machine, the export-import relationship will have very different implications. In these terms our external investments will greatly expand. Investments in Canada alone in 1976 will exceed the thirteen-billion figure which is the total of our last seven years of all foreign investments. Africa, of course, will be our main customer for capital funds.

Assume that dictators—communist, at the moment—tighten the belts of their slaves, and build a capital plant capable of vast production. Assume, as we rightly can, that new energies will replace man-hours of labor even in dictator lands. Is it not possible that the entire world may go free trade, since the slaves of dictators will become more interested in their leisure freedom-hours and hence less easily controllable by the dictators for their peculiar power purposes? In brief, can dictatorship work at all in a fission electronic leisure society?

In the meanwhile, we will be doubly alert to the maintenance of freedom in our market places of trade and business. Internally, the domination of our economic life is shifting from banks to insurance companies and union welfare funds. The welfare funds, now running into billions of dollars, will be subjected to supervision and regulation. If we are not careful, these funds will be subsumed by the government as part of an enlarged social security system.

Competition will be restored in the field of banking. In 1920 we had over thirty thousand banks; now we have fewer than fifteen thousand. Perhaps in 1920 they were too many and too weak; now with increased population and dispersal of people, they are far too few, except on the thesis of our repudiation of competition in the banking services of the nation. Our banks will be curtailed as to branches and deposits to increase competition among more separate entities. Men are not wise enough to supervise billions of dollars of other people's money in one company with hundreds of different branches. In one of our states there is a bank with more real power over the lives of the people than all the elected state officials have. Several banks have over a billion of deposits. By 1976, we will prevent further loss of competition through merger or sale, just as we will realize that when one bank dominates a state's financing facilities, that very fact points to statism. It is no answer that a particular giant is temporarily managed by angels with wisdom. To gamble on such continued wisdom is a hazard no democracy can afford.

The prestige value that was accorded to the early buccaneers will not attach with similar glamour to the businessmen infected with the gargantuan bug. The wiping out of the economic middle class will be looked on as an antisocial act.

The leader in the battle for economic freedom will be the Secretary of Commerce. He will desert his present role of protecting the giants, who no longer need protection except from their own stupidities. He will be the pro-

ponent of antitrust laws with teeth; he will watch for and
protect against antisocial mergers; he will urge that officials found guilty of price fixing shall be put on suspension
as unfit to direct other businesses in the future; he will
help educate small firms; he will defend competition
against the bottling up of the market place; he will preserve the independent banks by piercing the infirmities of
branch and chain banking. He will give aid to the money
and stock markets, without which new ventures cannot
procure necessary capital. He will end the circumvention
of the money markets by the insurance companies. As he
pursues the campaign for a nation of free businessmen,
the associations of so-called small businessmen will no
longer be clandestinely dominated by big business, which
today uses the dependent small companies as mere pup-
pets. With such a minister for Free Enterprise, our tax
laws will be revised so they will not discriminate—as they
do today—against the new enterprise, or against anything
less than a million-dollar company. Oversized businesses
will no longer live under special legislation which exempts
them, but penalizes every small company in its attempts
to accumulate capital.

Government, the largest buyer in our land (the federal government bought over fifty billion dollars' worth of
goods last year) will consciously assume the difficulties of
purchasing from thousands instead of from hundreds of
companies. The Secretary of Commerce will educate our
people, even the economically uninformed of the military.
He will show the waste and inefficiency of overbigness. He

will prove that security is diminished if our war potential rests only on the skills and profits of a hundred big companies. He will prove the cruel waste that occurs when one giant replaces a dozen smaller vital enterprises in which individuals or partners have intimate knowledge of daily operations.

The vertical trust will be broken up and competition will once more become significant. We are so far down the road toward complete concentration, that steel companies at times refuse to bid unless they get an order to produce the steel, fabricate the article and erect it. This kind of power in the market has wide collateral effects of most serious dimensions. The money market for underwritings in the millions is in fair shape, just as the borrower of a few thousand dollars can usually find banking facilities. But the business requiring semi-permanent capital, from $100,000 up to a million dollars, finds not only a meager and expensive market, but soon discovers that with our big branch-banking system, it must apply to a bank where the dominant giants in his own field sit as directors.

Today a third of moderate-size business in sound financial condition has difficulty in getting private capital funds. Our federal reports show that small business borrowers—assets under fifty thousand dollars—paid interest rates three times as high as those who borrow five million or over. How better can we wipe out free enterprise, which now survives only by the grace of the giants! Local community banks, informed of the needs of their home towns, will reverse such trends. No longer will the big cities, where the main offices of banks are located, suck out of the small towns major portions of the local deposits.

By 1976 the people of the world will be our customers, and we will buy from them. Our business youth will be educated abroad, and tens of thousands of businessmen will come here to examine our plant and scrutinize our methods. The more we grow in the spirit of free enterprise, the more our commerce will be integrated with the world, even though statism is on the increase elsewhere. Our imports of eight billions of food and minerals will be more than doubled, despite synthetics and the substitutes created by science. New commodities, new metals, new chemicals, new atoms will help stabilize the world markets for trade, and create the basis for currency convertibility. We will view as puny our present 2,300 companies which have controlling interests in 7,500 foreign enterprises in an amount that exceeds 10 billion dollars. We will look back with amazement to a time like the present when our major foreign investments were in oil. If, as a recent government report indicated, we only double our income by 1976, we will have at least 15 billion for investment. The people of the world will, during the next decades, seek capital equipment. We can produce it and we can finance the purchasers. And as we so export, political and economic stability will accompany each shipment. This kind of international business cannot be compared to the dominating influences of selling finished products to the consumers of other nations. The world trade we enter will liberate other peoples to create their own industrial plants, and produce what their raw materials indicate as necessary for the greatest economy. Thus they will reach a point of budget balancing.

Just as we are a race of gadgeteers, we also seem to have money-making aptitudes. Such aptitudes will not diminish, but will find different outlets as values of life blossom and expand. Today 18,000 of us *earn* over $100,-000 a year, and 200,000 take home between $25,000 and $50,000 a year. But these are only rainbow numbers. After taxes they look very different. In 1976, with inheritance taxes still remaining at rates up to 80 per cent, our business genius will find less compensation in big personal earnings and far more in the prestige value of better qualities of goods produced. The businessman of the next decade, to make a contribution comparable to Henry Ford's short-day-more-pay thesis, will be the one who tackles our distribution wastes. More than half of all cost goes into distribution. The automatic vending machines (now close to two billion sales, even including one selling worms for fishermen), self-service stores, direct shipments to consumer, localized area production plants, are all signs of hope. Refrigeration will improve so that sea food will not be limited to waterfront areas. By 1976 we may be able to buy at our stores goods not trebly wrapped in unopenable cellophane. Much of the hokum of advertising will disappear as our people find new and better values than vanity.

The tax rates will have democratized not only ownership of business, but of necessity will create new techniques for expression of the will and desire of the stockholders. The concept of bankruptcy court proceedings for large corporations will be a thing of the past. This outmoded device had values when a bankrupt company could be auctioned for sale before many buyers. Today there are few such sales. The only effect of bankruptcy of a giant company is a shift of control, and changes in proportion of earnings and liquidation values among classes of stock- or bondholders. There will be no issues of bonds, those silly papers that carry definite due dates for payment with receiverships as alternatives. Rather will all the protections of a bond be incorporated in a preferred stock. The impact of this change will show only in the loss to lawyers and accountants of the present judicial gravy, since on the failure of the company the preferred stock certificates will call for the shifts of control now ordered for bonds after years of court management. Bankruptcy, a drain on our economy, produces no income to the bankrupt, and is an antiquated concept with little application to properties too large to find a competitive market of buyers.

Leadership of business seems to be steering us toward ever shoddier goods, less distinguished products—and statism. I still think we can avoid such a disaster. But if we do, and are to go on to higher standards of living and of individual freedom, managers of industry will have to become leaders of society. They then will be of the elite who gain creative joy from their daily jobs and responsibilities.

If big business is to be made still bigger, fewer boys can be presidents of companies. Managerial positions, even with power and high pay, never provide the satisfactions derived from running one's own enterprise. If we can reverse the trend and regain competition, our machines of production in time will be manned by people who acquire honor and prestige from contributing goods of quality to a discriminating public.

Chapter 7

THE HOME AND FAMILY OF 1976

BY 1976 OUR INCOME WILL BE MORE THAN DOUBLED IN present dollars. Our population will increase only about 20 per cent, and our working hours will be reduced by at least 25 per cent. These three hearty events will of course have dramatic impact on the home and the family.

Today we have over forty-five million dwelling units. Nearly one half of these were built before 1920 and only 13 per cent after 1945. About 40 per cent of all our dwellings are classified in various reliable reports as "dilapidated," even though two million families rent or own a second vacation abode. Nearly one sixth have no piped running water, 15 per cent no kitchen sink, 20 per cent no mechanical refrigeration.

But we are truly two countries in this sphere. The rural population lives with less modern equipment, but also with far less congestion. It is for others to evaluate the effects on family life of the new conveniences compared to the destruction of privacy in overcrowded cities. All will agree that many family conflicts could be avoided or at least made bearable if there were room for privacy. For the teen-agers—in their struggle to get away from parental controls—the city street corners appear often to be more attractive than a home without a private room. It is difficult enough to become an adult even with privacy. The widespread development of boys' and girls' clubs are in part an answer to the inadequate space in our homes. It would not be difficult to argue that a private room is of more value than a dishwasher or a flush toilet. Without more and better housing, all of the emotional congestion that thrives in our crowded homes of today will be accentuated, as men and women work shorter hours and spend more time in their homes.

In depicting the trends of the future, the gap in facilities of, and attitudes between rural and urban folk must be kept in mind even though, by 1976, in mechanical facilities the two will nearly approximate each other. To illuminate these differences today, it might be noted that 92 per cent of urban and only 30 per cent of rural farm people enjoy flush toilets, while the number of families occupying and owning their own homes in small cities and on farms is at least five times as great as in the big cities.

With respect to appliances and gadgets, our homes will be unrecognizable, in 1976, by the people of today. We are on the march toward mechanized homes; by 1976, without acceleration in the present rate of installation, all housing will be fully supplied with basic plumbing. Even cooking facilities are improving. For example, only about one fifth of our homes still use coal or wood for cooking fuel as compared to one third in 1940.

Who owns these homes? In 1930, 42 per cent of urban and 52 per cent of farm and rural nonfarm homes were owner occupied. Twenty years later, in 1950, the percentages were close to 50 and 60 respectively, figures which seem surprisingly high to city folk as to urban home ownership and unbelievably low for the farm homes.

One way to see what our homes of today look like is to list some of the items of consumer capital goods which are of relatively recent development:

      96% have radios
      94% have electric lights
      75% have washing machines
      69% have telephones
      59% have vacuum cleaners
      47% have television
      33% have electric heaters
      29% have mixers
      24% have electric ranges
      11% have freezers
       9% have ironing machines
       3% have garbage disposal units
       3% have dishwashers
       1% have air conditioning

In 1940 only 83 per cent had radios, only 17 per cent had television, and only 78 per cent had electric lights.

Moreover, nearly three million vacuum cleaners, one million electric stoves and 340,000 air-conditioning units were sold in the single year 1952.

The mechanization of the home is well advanced, but the non-working mother with two children still is a fully occupied worker at home. The present estimate of a sixty-hour work-week is no exaggeration. The home apparatus of 1976 will greatly reduce this labor, although much will depend on the spending habits of the family unit. The percentage spent on housing now has decreased substantially, though we spend more for household equipment and its operations.

Although each statistician is devoted to his own pet set of figures, there is general agreement that in 1909 we spent roughly 30 per cent of our income on food, liquor and tobacco. By 1950 this grew to 34 per cent, and during the war when other items were not available, the figure was 37 per cent. What is far more significant is that our eating habits have changed. For example, in the period 1935-1939, we ate, on an average, 126 pounds of meat and 152 pounds of potatoes per year. By 1951 we ate more meat (141 pounds) and less potatoes (114 pounds). Egg eating went from 298 eggs per capita to 406 in the same period, and we doubled our chicken consumption. Bread purchases have shown substantial declines. The per capita consumer purchases of wheat dropped in the past quarter century from 230 pounds a year to 130.

The switch to ready-made food has been more obvious. Since 1947, frozen food production has quadrupled, with orange juice accounting for 20 per cent of all pound-age. However, in family units with an income of over $5,000, the use of canned food (except baby food) de-creases. The percentage of alcoholic beverages consumed has not materially increased. Until recently cigarette smoking was on the increase, and the average smoker laid out about $100 for tobacco per year. Each baby means, on the average, $100 worth of purchases at the drugstore. Eating in restaurants is a rather recent development, with purchases for food and beverages outside of the home run-ning about 25 per cent of the total spent on food.

Clothing gives some surprising information. In con-stant 1935-39 dollars we spent for clothing $65.74 apiece in 1929; $77.99 in 1944, and in 1949 were back down to $67.22. Thus while incomes rose, the per cent spent for clothing fell. The women's clothing budget shows that only in large communities do women spend a greater share of the family budget on clothing than do the men. But dresses under $6.00 accounted for 55 per cent of the total in 1946 and only 40 per cent in 1948. Adjusted to real dollars the shift is interesting, and might indicate a greater appreciation of quality, a resistance to the shoddy.

The expenditure no longer peculiar to women—toilet articles—rose from $400,000 in 1909 to over 1½ billion dollars last year. The average woman spent $4.05 on cos-metics in 1939 and $8.89 in 1947, with the increase show-ing up mainly in the war years, and mostly among women of low-income groups. Barber and beauty shops number close to 200,000 and take in close to a billion dollars a year.

To round out some odds and ends of the favor with which we appraise various personal commodities, a list prepared by the Department of Commerce may raise some amused comment:

What Civilians Spent in 1952

Total personal consumption expenditures—
$218,130,000,000*

(This is over three times the amount spent in 1939, and 177% more than consumers spent in 1929.)

Among Individual Items:

$254,700,000	Chewing Gum
234,990,000	Greeting Cards
196,590,000	Cough & Cold Items
145,270,000	Aspirin & Aspirin Compounds
129,640,000	Laxatives & Cathartics
107,450,000	Shampoos
65,120,000	Home Permanent Kits & Refills
48,530,000	Toilet Water & Cologne
42,980,000	Foot Products

* U. S. Department of Commerce, "Survey of Current Business," National Income Number, July 1953, Table 30, p. 23; 1929—$78,-761,000,000; 1939—$67,466,000,000.

All other figures from "Drug Topics," August 10, 1953 issue. Published by Topics Publishing Co., Inc., New York, N. Y.

37,910,000	Stomach Sweeteners
35,870,000	Hand Lotions & Creams
28,360,000	Mouth Washes & Gargles
26,580,000	Playing Cards
18,920,000	Nail Polish & Enamel
15,850,000	Elastic Stockings
7,400,000	Dog & Pet Medicaments
6,140,000	Hair Medicaments
4,330,000	Eye Lotions & Washes
3,300,000	Waveset Preparations

Within our present cultural standards, there seems to be little proof of any correlation between happiness and the installation of new household equipment. In the competition for increased comfort and leisure for the housekeepers, the desire for new appliances—mainly labor saving—rests on more than keeping up with the Joneses. However, the limits of purchase of household equipment can be estimated. As against fifty million family income-earning units today, there will be about ten million more in 1976 to be supplied with equipment, plus the already existing homes to be fully equipped. In 1950, as a people we spent about 10 per cent of our incomes on heavy durables, including automobiles, TV, refrigeration, et cetera. Cars alone took over one half of this sum, and in cities where TV had favorable reception, it used up another 2 to 3 per cent. But our architects, often throttled by contractors, put up homes long outdated, and children grow up in a décor a generation behind their times, since the house reflects the era of the marriage.

Above all, we need more and better homes. No matter what stupidities may delay the improvements, there can be no doubt that with an 800-billion-dollar gross national product in 1976, the American home will enjoy more space and conveniences. The tendency toward smaller units is evident. In 1890 there was an average of 4.93 people to a household, by 1930 this was reduced to 4.11, and by 1951 to 3.34. Today, most people live in detached homes (64 per cent of all dwelling units) and the median number of rooms is about 4½ to a family.

There are those, however, who contend that the ambition to improve the home in physical terms will never be satisfied. I believe that the defenders of this position are overlooking the impact of new values which leisure will create. The urgent need to buy a new car every two or three years—at least long before its effective use expires —has already turned the corner. The automobile business will run into a sorry economic mess, primarily because it will be unable to keep on fooling our people into the trade-in of an old car because of a bit more chrome on the fender, or a new futile gadget. We now see the second-hand car market murdering the new-car business.

At the moment, we have an extraordinary susceptibility to novelties, gadgets and often worthless but fabulously titled advertised apparatus. Long before 1976 we will have better homes and equipment—but not to impress the neighbors. A small car, easily parked, requiring less gas and upkeep, and a smaller garage, will save a family enough to take care of that trip to Africa. Many home appliance firms will advertise their wares in terms of savings which the consumer can then put into a graduate education for a child, or new fishing equipment. Even books will be preferred to the present joy of showing off to friends and relations. The greatest single saving in family spending will result from self-satisfying uses of leisure time.

Such observations do not imply a static world in homemaking. There will be constant changes and improvements. The competition of home appliances will shift from the tinsel and chrome standards to factors of more real value. To be sure, homemaking in itself is one of the great creative arts of man. Little can people of our culture understand the satisfactions of the French housewife who spends what seems to us an inordinately high per cent of her weekly budget on food, and very little on new kitchen gadgets. Many a French housewife dies with the same copper pots and pans which were given to her at the time of her marriage.

There is no indication that our women will turn to drabness or monotony in the home. Rather is it likely that our kitchens will carry much more color back of the new electronic oven which will bake food in a matter of seconds. Charcoal or hickory flavors will be wafted to smoke meats. Push-button apparatus for ice in various forms, magnetic holds for canisters, flour sifting operated by motor, et cetera, are in the offing. All cabinet, ice box and stove doors will slide open by mere touch or by photoelectric eye, and above all, the height for working and shelf space will have some relation to the muscles in women's backs. Electric insulations will fend off dirt and noise. Ice boxes will be only for keeping food cool, while vacuums will preserve our edibles. Homes will be heated by atom or solar heat, or by the heat pump which draws heat from underground. All our power and heat will come into the home by way of the ether, with the entire removal of all wire and telephone poles which mar the scenery and are so expensive to keep in repair. In fact, the light and power for the home will be so cheap that it won't pay to meter it. But all these inventions have only one purpose: more time for a full, rich personal and family life.

Homes are more than brick and mortar. They are the setting for family cooperation and individual privacies. The center of the home is, in a sense, the kitchen. This is where so much time must be spent. Despite the ideas of a few sophisticated Americans who know little of our national ways of life, never in our history were more than 3 per cent of homes fortunate enough to have, living in, regular domestic help. During the height of immigration—in the days of a glutted labor market— fewer than one million homes had a living-in cook, maid or general housekeeper. But today more people are earning money in the domestic field than ever before. The part-time nurse, part-time cook or maid, and above all, the baby sitter, are working with a dignity and respect quite remote from the old relation of "menial" and "master." But no matter how life will be organized, the running of the home for a mother with one or two children will be a full job. The vast increase of cookbook sales in recent years clearly indicates the change in the creative attitude toward the art of cooking, and also reveals that present-generation housewives did not learn cooking from their mothers. Increasing development of group nurseries, exchange of services between neighboring parents, and a much further developed non-living-in maid service, paid by the hour, will give relief to the housewife-mother. The employment of college graduates as baby sitters is already a revolutionary sign of change. But even more important will be the active participation of the husband-father in this homemaking, where the working male will cheerfully undertake chores which he formerly disdained. A score of years ago the father was insulted if the wife asked him to dry or wash the dishes. Until the offspring were in the talking stage Papa, with superior airs of a kind befitting an employer, said, "Let Mama do it." The wife of the future will not use her man only to empty the garbage cans. Rather will she wait for him with many chores which can be shared with satisfaction.

The prestige value of getting something better than the neighbor thrives only in a culture of empty lives, or among those who have only recently become financially secure. This can best be evidenced by looking at the rich who have owned inherited wealth for several generations. In those homes the old, not-used-up auto, the old-fashioned bookcase and furniture are retained during succeeding generations. By 1976 all of our homes will be thoroughly equipped in such a way as to reduce the susceptibility of the public to the inducements of advertising agents. The rare, the different, the distinguished—and not necessarily the newest or the most expensive—will have a profound effect on the purchasing public. Articles newly conceived, and produced to reduce or sweeten the work in the home, will be written about in the press and magazines as news stories. In this culture of 1976, uniformity will be held in disdain, and we will see, aside from a few basic necessities, more individuality expressed in homemade products.

This shift will occur, and is occurring, so quietly and subtly as to be scarcely discernible. One of the reasons for our national ignorance in this field arises from the fact that newspapers, magazines, radio and television, in our present distorted economic market place, only keep us aware of advertised items. The spending of millions by amateur stargazers or geologists seems to merit little news comment and certainly no concern which manufactures telescopes, shovels or picks appropriates sufficient funds to advertise over press, radio or television.

When leisure was the prerogative only of wealth, new luxuries first found their way into home use via the newly rich, who displayed possession to garner esteem. Then mass advertising used as a motif the slogan: "You, too, can dress or look or eat like the rich." The peak of this false kind of living was clearly evidenced in the public revulsion toward a television producer who advertised that you were a social outcast if your children were without television!

By 1976 practically every family will have one building artisan, and in addition one person who enjoys painting the new bookcase or weaving the new tapestry. The present eighteen million home gardens will spread to every home outside the big cities. With the new concentrated chemicals of the soil, window boxes will partially compensate city folk for their distance from the land. Clothing, homemade, will produce beauty presently precluded by mass styling. We already know that the so-called stylists do not create styles. The only credit they deserve is that they intuitively interpret the political and economic forces of their time. The length of women's skirts for forty years has varied, except for one brief exception, with the stock market; beige came into popularity because we were overstocked with khaki dyes; hoop skirts went out with the inconvenience of boarding trains; black stockings for women disappeared in World War I when the Germans had a virtual monopoly on black dyes, and the men's sport clothes business expanded only when we reached a week-end leisure economy.

Men's clothing, even more than the garb of women, will undergo a revolution. Males will employ more color, more individuality and far more comfort. The tie and the hat are on the way out. The male seven-ply collar and coat in warm weather are already recognized as absurdities— with men approaching closer to wearing a blouse as the basic garment.

Women in trousers are no longer an oddity, and I doubt if high heels, or toes painted red showing through women's shoes, will sexually excite many males; while the naming of the so-called ten best-dressed women of the year will be recalled in 1976 as ridiculous as the listing of Mrs. Astor's Four Hundred. The synthetic textiles purchased for home sewing into garments will dry quickly, permit moisture to be absorbed, take dyes easily and have a softer feel than so-called natural fabrics. They won't need ironing, without which, I am told, a woman's life is paradise!

Only a few basic items will be standardized in order to produce low costs through mass production. But beyond these items—mostly home capital goods—the Jones family will be put out of business, not because unorthodoxy has any value per se, but because the individuality of each home will express itself in its own unique way. And of one thing we can be certain—creative people living the full life in family homes will act and look in as many different ways as there are families. If one home has a rocking chair in the kitchen because the family likes it there, they will have it there even though the neighbor has one in the bedroom.

The independence of the housewife from phony standards is already affecting one of the great burdens of our economy—packaging. Although we will not go so far as to tote unwrapped loaves of bread on our streets, as in France, by 1976 the cellophane, tinfoil, thrice-wrapped and super-packaged piece of cheese will have given way to unostentatious wrapping of cheese, sold, in consequence, at a price where the wrapping costs less than the commodity itself. Packaging will be for the purpose of protection and not to impress the neighbors.

More important to the family are the clearly indicated abolition of the three great wastes: rust, moths, and the common cold. The removal of these three extreme burdens will lift our economy as few other inventions can possibly do.

But homes are less than homes unless there be children. And here we must face up to the fact that one half of all the children are in one sixth of the homes—homes which have only one tenth of the income. The history of the folkways of man can be seen in terms of the toys fashioned by men and women for the children of the next generation. It is no mere coincidence that in our land the military figures have given way to building blocks, mechanos and all sorts of chemical and electrical sets. Dolls and housekeeping toys now purchased only for girls will also be used by the male youngsters of 1976, just as more and more girls will enjoy the scientific toys heretofore deemed exclusively fit for males. In the new home where the father will no longer "run" the home, and where all members of the family will engage in joint as well as separate creative play, the male child will not be ashamed of playing with dolls, and cooking and home-simulating toys. The word "sissy" will disappear from the vocabulary. By 1976, toys will be less artificial because the environment of the home will induce painting, writing, music, carving, poetry, pottery-making, and those innumerable pleasant and simple, but highly satisfying, outlets for man's self-expression. Nor does this mean the incorporation in the home of tense standards of competition.

During the war we invented the phrase "doorkey kids"—children sent out to school or to play, with the doorkey tied around their necks, while the mothers went to work. This extreme symbol of the breakdown of the real purpose of the home is not unrelated to juvenile delinquency, and the increase of resistance of children to parents. The new home will have little relation to such an atmosphere.

A new kind of solid family will arise. Parents with leisure will have only such number of children as they consciously desire. The myth of the "love child" will be exploded. More of our children will at that time be love children. More parents will have more children and more parents will have fewer children. The norm will be the suitable, and desired, number.

The marriage age is already shifting. In the decade of 1940 to 1950 the marriage age of men went down from 24.3 to 22.6 years. And obviously in a society with a trend toward a doubling of per capita income, the economic barriers to early marriage will be further reduced.

Knowledge of contraception will be translated into profoundly new attitudes toward the home and children. The marriages our young people will design and control will buffet the adjustments which now too often end in divorce. The marriage age differential, now justified on other than economic grounds, will diminish.

But the really important potentials of new leisure and wider knowledge will be in parent-child attitudes in the everyday life of the family. In the days before leisure, sons saw little of their fathers except on farms, or in the case of men who owned small retail stores. Estrangement of father and sons has been a real factor in the collapse of the family as a traditional force of social value, and in the rise of so-called juvenile delinquency.

The 1976 father and son will spend time together—at play—and sons will get a healthier idea of family life when mother and father share duties once relegated to one sex or the other. Even today mothers are challenged as sauce concocters or diaper changers by fast-learning fathers. When fathers have time to grow up with their sons, we will see less of the infantile attitudes of superiority stemming from the fact that today the boy often knows more about making a radio or fixing an engine than his sire.

Daughters always were more intimately aware of mother's family duties and lived with the image of female adulthood before them. Such intimacy may account for the earlier emotional development of girls; when the boys have the same sort of image in their fathers, the delayed emotional maturity of men may be overcome.

The intimacy of family life in 1976 also will encourage the handing-on process which is as essential as the need of the next generation to march further than the past one. Parents will have time and inclination to keep up with the new excitements of youth. Continuity of traditions can then accompany growth and change, instead of being in conflict as they so often are now.

At the other end of the family cycle, too, we shall see changes. As men and women marry nearer the same age, the tragic waste of widowhood will be reduced, especially as the mortality tables may not continue to favor female survival when the tenser male burdens are shifted to the new machines. But in any case, the experience of having lived a full and rich family life will reduce the loneliness of the widowed; there will be no more of the false idea that a new adventure in marriage is disloyalty to the deceased spouse, and the years added at the tail end of life will be emotionally enriched.

Another factor to be taken into account is the desire of women to engage in work outside of the home. In 1776 men did the marketing and shopping, taking to town for barter the butter and eggs, and the woven goods made by the wife. Only recently women took over from men the retail buying tasks of the family. Women today are the shoppers, the buyers. But in addition, there are now nineteen million working women in our land—five times as many as in 1890, six and a half million more than in 1940, and three million more than immediately after World War II. In 1941, 24 per cent of American housewives held jobs. By 1953 this had grown to 30 per cent. In 1940 one third of all working women were married; by 1953 more than half of all working women were married. It must be noted, however, that only one per cent of all working women earn more than $5,000, and more than 80 per cent get less than $2,500 per year.

In 1976 the reasons for married women with children going out to work will be quite different from the causes which motivate them now. No longer will they want to work because housework bores them. The pressure for adequate family spending power will be less severe. The present desire to get outside of a female environment into a male one will be less imperative since the males will have shorter work days and will spend more time with their wives and children.

Home-tending women will go out to work if they have skills in those occupations which supply creative satisfactions—making of machines, research, teaching, dealing with First Amendment material, and the arts and sciences. They will not seek money-making jobs for the money but because of satisfactions.

With the new push-button economy, the role of women in the research, arts and science fields will by 1976 be scarcely differentiated from that of the male. Shorter hours in industry will more readily permit the mother-housekeeper to take on some outside activity. On the other hand, the new joint father-mother home will develop such excitements that mothers of young children will find their highest outlets for creative energies in that most difficult of all chores: the nurturing of children adjusted to their environment and conscious of their own capacities and limitations.

Innumerable minor changes will affect the home. Stores open during the hours when industry as such will not be operating, the impact of tax revision so as no longer to deter women from working, the rearrangement and size of the new houses, the relation of parents to schools, the expansion of adult education, the highly satisfying occupation of serving on community committees dealing with community problems—these and other intangibles will affect, change and enrich the family in the home.

Chapter 8

EDUCATION AND THE RICH LIFE

AS A PEOPLE WE TALK AS IF WE TAKE PRIDE IN EDUCATION.
Many parents make substantial sacrifices to send their
children to high schools and colleges. Those who seek political office use high-sounding phrases to refer to our own
schools as compared to those of foreign nations. In words
—and in words alone—we worship the Little Red School
House.

Democracy—particularly when applied as a way of
life over a large and widespread population—cannot be effective without education—that is, literacy, critical capacity and means of communicating ideas. We have licked
the mechanics of communication, but education suffers in
unAmerican fashion.

It is depressing and bewildering to take stock of the
horrible mess in which our educational system flounders.
Thousands of intelligent men and women of good will

and lofty ideals have described and protested our short-comings over the past half century, all to no avail. We haven't a respectable plant or enough teachers; not to mention the absence of goals for the educational content. We are suffering from an obvious historical confusion. In our natural desire to provide educational facilities for ·all, we were satisfied with quantity irrespective of quality. We seem to have transferred all of the worst features of big business to the mass education of our youth. We adopted the gospel of The Biggest and not The Bestest.

It is true that we have reduced illiteracy to less than 3 per cent in a world of 70 per cent illiteracy. But at the same time we find steadily rising proportions of juvenile crime and parental delinquency. We increase the number of students each year and learn that drug addiction among adolescents has become a serious problem in the large cities. Every hamlet has a little red schoolhouse, but we read fewer books than do the people of other equally literate nations. We facilitate attendance by free buses and free lunches, and find at the same time tawdriness increasing in magazines, movies and television.

It is as if we judged education only by numbers; as if statistics alone were a proper basis for pride. When we boast that twenty-five million go to elementary schools we fail to mention that primary education is increasingly on a two- or even three-shift basis.

Schools cannot avoid being the matrix of a democratic culture. Although press, radio, film and churches are serious and important influences in social attitudes, education must always be the keystone. Teaching must affect these other instruments, rather than allow them to establish our standards of taste and the directions of our curiosities. Before 1976 our educational system will contest much that appears in the market place of thought, and eventually we will even educate a new crop of owners of our communication system, and the sponsor-advertisers who dominate much that comes into our lives in non-school hours. Our present problem is how to raise education to its real duty of inculcating critical capacity in our youth—without boiler-plating their minds.

In the first of the two sectors of our problem—the sufficiency of rooms and teachers on the one hand, and the quality of instruction on the other—one would assume that with our genius for creating brick and mortar we would have done a respectable job. Likewise one would suppose that we would have established a labor market sufficient to corral teachers in sufficient numbers to meet the growing demand. Neither is true. Hence I find no optimism for the future by looking at the present, although even the pessimist must say, "We can't do worse."

The dimensions of the business of education are so fantastic as to becloud the consideration of what kind of education we want in our fast changing democracy. The enrollment of all elementary students—including private as well as public—exceeds twenty-five million, more than all the inhabitants of Denmark, Belgium and Holland. Secondary school attendance—nearly seven million—is double the population of Ireland. In 1960 this total figure will equal forty-five instead of thirty-two million. And by 1976 we will need to double the number of teachers and classrooms. These increases will result not only from normal population increments but from extension of school years through high school. For every three students in high school today there will be five in 1965 and at least seven in 1976.

But at the moment we are short 400,000 classrooms, not to mention the fact that seven million pupils go daily to firetraps for instruction. The brick and mortar shortage in 1976 will run as high as 600,000 rooms unless we come to grips with the problem.

Pupils can be educated, in Mark Hopkins fashion, by placing a student on one end of a log and a teacher on the other—provided only that there be teachers. Now, we have only one million teachers. We require for this year 160,-000 additional elementary schoolteachers, but fewer than 40,000 are entering the profession. To provide for the secondary school attendance, even at our present inadequate standards, we turned out 86,000 teachers in 1950, 73,000 in 1951, 61,000 in 1952, and only 55,000 in 1953. More pupils—fewer teachers—not enough rooms, even though by 1976 we will need to treble our teaching force.

Public schools cost us less than ten billions last year, of which less than half went to teachers. We need five billions additional a year for each of the next few years just to catch up on the present severe shortages of equipment and teacher training. By 1960, with increased population and more years of study, we will face a budget of just ordinary decency in the amount of twenty billion dollars, and by 1976 the sum required will be close to thirty billion a year.

In 1920 we spent $50 a student for our public elementary and kindergarten schools. In 1948 we were up to $150 per capita. Higher education enrolled 600,000 in 1920 at a cost of $360 per student. In 1948 the enrollment of 2½ million cost $650 per capita. This so-called "improvement" represents a decline in real dollar costs viewed against modern educational techniques. Moreover, per capita cost has little overall meaning in an era when universities are running competitive student belts—competing primarily for numbers—some exceeding 40,000 and still soliciting more.

But the dollar cost per student tells only one part of the story. The real test of the value a society places on education is better seen in the per cent of total income employed. In the depression years, 1933-34, we spent over 4 per cent of our national income on education at all levels. With a greatly increased national income, we have gone down to about 2½ per cent of our national income.

The higher education enrollment shows a remarkable rise in women students in the past half century, to the point where presently women account for one third of the total. Of our 1,800 colleges and universities two thirds are private, one third public. At one time about one third of all students were financed by the federal government, the great G.I. subsidies; the federal government's contribution of nearly four billion included about three and three-fourths billion which came through the Veterans' Administration.

In 1900 we granted college degrees to 30,000; last year we graduated over 350,000. The private colleges are all semicharitable since about half of all tuition costs come from past and present benefactions. Corporation gifts and the federal government grants for research have kept many universities solvent and in business.

An oft overlooked educational facility is seen in the nearly four million students who take advantage of federally aided vocational classes—one fourth in agriculture, one fourth in trade and industry and one half in home economics. Toward this program the local governments contribute five dollars for each dollar supplied from Washington. In number of students California leads this list; Texas second and Georgia third.

We are justly indictable by the next generation for failing to supply schoolrooms and teachers, but what possible plea can we make to the true charge that the average school (elementary) teacher's salary is only about $2,800 a year, with 700,000 of our teachers without any job security?

Into this grim picture hope can only enter by a glance at our past. Man has only spent a very few minutes of his total history in the pursuit of knowledge. In fact, the opening story of that comparatively recent writing called the Old Testament, is a condemnation of knowledge. As I read Genesis, a couple—Adam and Eve—were offered peace, comfort and plenty, on one condition. They should never seek knowledge. It was because one of them—interestingly enough the woman—sought the fruits of knowledge that, according to this quaint myth, all men and all women were supposed to be condemned to misery and grief forever. In Genesis 6-5 we even read: "Every imagination of the thoughts of his heart was only evil continually." Thus emotional as well as intellectual curiosity was historically banned.

Such mandate for ignorance was not uniquely laid down by the ancient Jewish leaders. Prometheus—for his zeal to endow man with fire, the symbol of light as well as heat—was punished by Zeus, carried off to the Caucasian mountains to be bound to a mighty rock so that a great vulture could unceasingly tear at his liver. In like fashion, the folklore of many religions condemns all desire for education. That we overcame such enslaving tradition is quite miraculous.

It took hundreds of generations before the educated dared share the enrichment of knowledge with others. The religious leaders, the storytellers, the scribes, were in most cultures a band of monopolists in a closed union. They were reluctant to risk the impairment of their influence by the education of others. The flock must accept the Word. Questions are always a threat to the insecure who hope to hold power over the minds of others. It seemed safer to ban education than to educate man.

So that we do not adopt too chauvinistic an attitude, I note that the Madras System, under which students taught each other, was carried into England from India

in 1798, and may justly be called the progenitor of our
Free Public School System. To the crusade, in the early
eighteenth century, of Francis Place, conducted under the
slogan "Schools for All," we directly owe our own free
public schools. The then aristocracy of learning is best described by the approximate guess of historians that at the
time of the founding of our Republic only 25 per cent of
the 3,600,000 white folk in the Thirteen Colonies could do
more than read or write their own names. Women were
trained only for the needle and the spinet; and the 400,-
000 Negro slaves were not even considered educable. But
those who did read were deeply erudite, even though the
largest library of the period contained no more than four
thousand volumes. Education had a rare quality just because those who had knowledge also had leisure, and
hence the time for study and contemplation.

The hundred weekly gazettes of the period had an
average circulation of less than one thousand copies, but
the unquenchable thirst for knowledge was symbolized by
a local ordinance which provided that the reader of a
township newspaper, cooperatively subscribed to, should
not read the advertisements until all others had read the
news.

A half century after our nation was politically established, one of man's few revolutionary ideas began to
spread: Free public education. The long and bitter opposition against this concept was far greater than the more
recent fights against the minimum wage, or for child labor legislation. The aristocrats of the alphabet argued

that the minds of the masses were unfit for conceptual uses.

Originally, instruction was under the control of the clergy. Then gradually education was taken over by financial benefactors (replacing, maybe regrettably, the lotteries as sources of income). The colleges particularly were dominated by men better equipped to market stocks and bonds than inculcate scholarship. As a concomitant, instruction in theology slowly gave way to the teaching of economics and the sciences. In many institutions of higher learning the organized alumni, obviously a potential source of revenue, took power, often in the role of advocate of the status quo. Maybe the greatest feature of the Rockefeller grant to establish Chicago University was the exclusion of elected alumni from the Board of Trustees. The most active alumni are often those who stopped learning when they graduated, and thus as perpetual sophomores lead the alumni body—a body which with strong memories enjoys the recollection of college days as the never-to-be-relived protected era of their lives. The alumni leader was often the college idol of the athletic field, rather than the holder of a Phi Beta Kappa key. Colleges were used as symbols of intellectual snobbery, and a college degree for a time was little more than a token of Pop's desire for conspicuous expenditure, particularly the case with non-collegiate fathers.

The aristocracy of the learned of our early days created consistently high standards in primary education, the leaders of which were often men of great distinction.

Moreover, until the start of the nineteenth century, all education was carried on in units small enough for man to supervise and manage with an eye toward new pedagogical advances. But as we stepped forward with mass free compulsory primary education—with overflows such as the kindergarten at one end and the high school or junior highs at the other—the gap between college and all other sectors of the business of education increased. This gap was accented when the private lower and high schools had to meet the competition of public primary and secondary education. Nor did the more recent introduction of free or nearly free college education offered by city or state close the gap. The colleges had slight influence on the standards of instruction or courses at high schools, while the lower grades went their own way unrelated to high school processes. We lacked integration and often too much or too little pressure was exerted by the meaningless dogmas of college admission requirements. Those who directed education in college were isolated from elementary school education, and until recently were not in touch even with public high school objectives.

The conversion from private to public education brought into the picture political influences directed not by educators but by public office-seekers. Schools were big business and invited as managers those who knew more about finances than education. Scholars no longer directed. They became hired underlings. With the accent on educating boys more than girls, the sexual isolationism of education increased. Only recently have parents been tied into associations to express their democratic concern with the precious aspects of educating their offspring.

The feminist revolution of the past half century shows its impact on all parts of the education field. Over the past twenty-five years we find that more women than men have completed high school, but fewer attended college. More than 55 per cent of the degrees of teachers' colleges went to women. Women crashed all professions, and now there are twice as many in dentistry, nine times in engineering and 50 per cent more at the bar than in 1940. Ten thousand women took advantage of the G.I. educational grants.

To convert our sorry mess of today into schooling fit for a decent people, we must look to a few hopeful trends appearing in our long past history and a series of new approaches which, hopefully, will flow from our new leisure high-standard economy.

Three groups of people are directly involved: teachers, parents and children. The attitude of each of these groups will depend on the societal values which we as a nation place on education. For us to take intelligent action we must place education in a priority status in the spending of our wealth. We will realize that education pays off, even in dollars. A small dent in the numbers flowing through reformatories and prisons, a moderate reduction in the cost of policing against crime, a minimal saving in the cost of criminal courts, a decrease in the 700,000 people residing in our mental institutions—a combination of these factors or others which the reader may

select—will more than provide the funds needed for more
and better equipment, more and better trained teachers,
and will leave over ample funds for the servicing of those
who end their education all too soon, in order that they
may fill their full roles in our future democracy.

But it is the teaching group that is crucial for the
development of education, because the teachers who get
their training now will still be teaching in 1976. The parents and children will more readily change and grow with
the times.

All through our history little attention has been given
to the root of all education—the teaching of teachers. But
worse still, if a teacher was once trained, little thought
was given toward the modernization of the teacher's
mind. It is no exaggeration to say that some teachers still
teach from notes first proudly written a decade or more
ago. Unlike even the stodgy professions of law and medicine, teaching is remote from market-place competition.
Promotions scarcely are analogous to the testing of approval by clients or patients. In fact, the patients of teachers are seldom articulate or, if articulate, listened to. The
recent organized approval or disapproval of the parents
has been too slender and uninformed to be constructively
helpful. Nor were elementary teachers given the opportunity to reinvigorate themselves. The college staff, on the
other hand, was, generally speaking, granted a sabbatical
year for a mental refresher. Little did they need it compared to those who were dealing with very young, un-
formed minds in a society of growth and change. We will

in the future realize that the sound emotional development of youth requires more periodic reappraisal than does the collection of fresh knowledge for the older student. The elementary and high school staffs who entered our system in 1930 are the teachers of today. Only in the last decade have we admitted that teaching methods and approaches become quickly outdated and that teachers go stale if they are not constantly updated.

I doubt if the vast flow of new factual knowledge is anywhere near as great in quantity or quality as the new psychological pedagogic wisdom that has enriched our world since 1900. Much of the maladjustment of youth is chargeable to the school system of our day which, organized on the pedagogic theories of a previous generation, changed too little to meet the changing world.

If the teachers trained this year are to be any good in twenty years, they must be not only extraordinary people but part of a system that is not founded on the thesis that teaching is a static art. Particularly in the elementary schools, teachers will be given a sabbatical year to travel and to take courses to bring their teaching techniques up to date.

At the moment it takes as much as fifty years for a new pedagogical idea to creep into the public school system of a big city. In part, this is due to the type of people whom teaching has attracted. The profession will attract more of the best types in the new world of 1976. Teachers will gain in prestige and, with higher status, will be better paid. As we draw the lines more sharply between satisfying and dull occupations, teaching will rank up near the top with research and the arts and sciences. In fact, teaching the very young will be the most exciting, rewarding and delicate research undertaken by man.

The salaries of our teachers in elementary and secondary schools are pitifully low, judged by any standards, running in some states as low as $1,400 a year. Even college teachers have on the average been paid less than half the income of doctors and dentists. As against such shocking profiteering in our society it can be said that teaching has creative compensations as compared with working in any push button, belted factory. Teaching will always have far greater personal rewards. The present longer vacations for teachers will, however, get closer to the one month with pay which will be generally accepted by all industry. Teachers of 1976 will be paid more than entrepreneurs, salesmen of brooms or manicurists in beauty parlors. The principal of a school will earn more than the head of a funeral parlor and a college professor may be paid as much as a left fielder.

But mere money reward by itself will not inevitably attract the kind of teachers we need. They will be better selected and better trained. Teaching the teachers will acquire a professional status above that of any college faculty membership. The head of a teachers' college will be better known and more respected than the president of any university. This will happen because the teachers developed by one generation determine the zeal and mental agility of the student of the next. We will seek dynamic personalities rather than people who are merely adept in cataloguing factual knowledge. Modern psychology is sufficiently advanced to help us in such personality diagnosis. Colleges will consciously participate in such a program as an insurance for better applicants in the next decades. Changes in this direction are presently within view. The professor is no longer depicted as the absent-minded ninny who forgets his glasses or his umbrella. The denegation of thought by the attempted ridicule of a phrase such as "brain trust" failed. The anti-intellectualism of McCarthyism is only a subject of passing concern. The science of teaching is on the march, and as we raise the prestige of scientists, teaching will also get a new look. Parents will no longer think that anyone can be a teacher.

In 1787 women teachers, except in the Dame Schools, were scarcely dreamed of. By 1870, 40 per cent of all teachers in primary and secondary schools were women. In 1910, only one out of five teachers was male; by 1920 the figure shrank to one out of seven. Then with the severe economic depression more men entered this great profession because the financial rewards declined comparatively less than the pay in most other jobs. By 1949, although teachers' salaries had once more declined in comparative terms, men still accounted for 20 per cent of all teachers. In the single term of 1949-50 the increase in men over the previous year was 18 per cent, with only 3 per cent increase of women. I find no psychological or biological arguments that point to preferable value of female over male pedagogy. Nor is there much provable validity for universities and colleges adopting sex distinctions in student bodies.

By 1976 these artificial, though historically explicable, postures will disappear and we will no longer be able to ask: Why is English usually taught by women, and history by men?

Education today is quite non-competitive as between institutions. If the schools had plants beyond the student applications, then institutions would compete in different terms with each other. Of course it might be said that such competition would be for quantity instead of quality, with an over-all lowering of standards in all institutions. This argument gains some support by analogy to the decline in quality of our press where subscribers and advertisers are competed for at an increasing pressure on taste, truth and dignity. But education is presently far removed from any competitive, critical or effective audience reaction, and our new society will provide critical forces in the direction of quality and content, not just quantity.

Public school children and their parents usually have no choice. The child must go to the school in the neighborhood or face a truant officer. The parent cannot shop for a public school. He can only shop for a home near a good school. A handful of private schools—particularly secondary—are corrected mainly by records of their success or failure to train for entrance examinations for certain colleges. Since, until recently, the parents had no judgment as to value of the education purchased for their sons other than the admission or refusal of entrance to a college, the schools suffered from the absence of that kind of continuing daily critical judgment which commodities receive in the ordinary market places of commerce.

In brief, education sorely needs competition—not for numbers but in ideas. And such competition will come first and mainly from parents and alumni. Since alumni are usually also parents, they will be peculiarly concerned with the quality of the education of their own children, without too much pride in mere quantity of output. In fact, some alumni will appreciate that quantity is often antithetical to quality.

In the upper education field, colleges have for several decades relied heavily on their alumni (and a few non-alumni parents) but the reliance has been mostly for dollars. In 1950 these institutions graduated a quarter of a million men and women whose devotion to education and to an alma mater made them susceptible to financial pleas. The private colleges—two thirds in number, with 50 per cent of the students and nearly 50 per cent of the income —are starting to realize that the alumni are capable of supplying more than dollars. Some colleges appreciate that even the money plight might be aided by educational ideas and that some alumni might possess ingenuity in that field.

Colleges and universities will be catapulted into violent changes. With one more turn of the inheritance tax wheel, large personal bequests will come to an end. Already most colleges would be out of business except for government and corporate dollar support. As with community charity, the median amount of gifts is declining at a rate faster than the increase of income-tax rates. Thus, higher education has increasingly tried to rely on widespread alumni help. But this help is of slight avail in making up the deficit in the long run. Endowments in 1940 provided 25 per cent of such educational income. By 1950 this was down to 10 per cent, while costs of universities have increased 50 per cent, and of private colleges 70 per cent in the past ten years.

I anticipate a complete change in the leadership of alumni associations, and suggest it will arise because of the new interest of parents in the education of their own children. Men, the financial supporters of colleges, will see more of their sons at home, and this alone will create new attitudes toward education.

In 1950 there were one thousand citizen committees concerned with education. Now this number exceeds eight thousand. Parent-teacher groups now have eight million members, double the number of 1946. Thus, for the first time, our nation has in the making a mechanism for continuous, concerned and effective criticism of our schools. The growth in the power of these groups will revolutionize elementary education in the first instance, and will finally upset the educational complacency of even those colleges which have waiting lists. The present accented interest of certain alumni to get undeserved entrance to, or retention of their sons in a college will have to stand up against the desire of other alumni to gain better education for their offspring.

Adolescent students, though vocal in their complaints, are presently without much influence in keeping the teaching force alert. Hence parents will pass on reactions of students to faculties. It will take time before the results are apparent, for many parents must first learn that the education they received twenty years earlier is not necessarily the best, in fact is necessarily *not* the best. Education will be less stereotyped and will reach a healthy state of constant change and growth. It will be retooled not just every year or two as is the case with bathtubs or breakfast food packages, but every day and every hour. The hallmark of education will be its capacity to change, unlike the enduring branded trademarks on commodities.

I lay great stress on what the reorganized home—of financial comfort and ample time for spiritual satisfactions —will contribute to our school system. Some parents will be grumblers, some dilettantes, but many will become students of the process of education. Most will integrate their own expansion of knowledge and the considerations of emotional adjustments in the homes with what goes on in the schools. Eagerness to go to school will increase. We will reverse the present disturbing influence of homes on schools so that homes will integrate the education at home with the education in the schools. Today there is often an antagonism between the two.

More parents will be concerned with teacher training and classroom overcrowding. The saddest commentary about the elementary education of our day is that few of us can name even one outstanding person in the primary school field. A mediocre professor at a liberal arts college is likely to have a greater reputation than the leading teacher of the six-year-olds in any school of our nation.

As a result of our new leisure life, more home-working mothers will enter the teaching profession. Thus we will completely reverse the recent folkway which foreclosed teaching to married women. Parents will seek appointments to school boards, and will work with school authorities, as is the case in thousands of small towns today. In the bigger cities the school boards will be broken up. No group of five or seven people is competent to run education for a population of 25,000 or more. In cities like New York there will be a school board for each assembly district and eventually, by 1976, for each school. Then we will see competition of ideas in the "knowledge business." Just as people now move out of big cities because they hear of better schools in suburbs, so in the big cities we will either open up competition so that parents can send their children to a school other than one in the immediate neighborhood—save only for travel burdens on the children—or people will move to that part of the city which affords the best education. Thus comparative public critical judgments will provide the competition which our rejuvenated teaching force will welcome. The stodgy and rutted part of the teaching force will be competitively compelled by parental demonstration, rather than by political forces, to keep the teaching of ideas to the young in tune with our changing and richer life.

To assure the independence of public college education in 1976, we have a formula at hand fully tested in our courts. Education will be the fourth separate division of government, as in Minnesota today. Such structural separation of powers will be adopted in other states, by statutes or by tradition. This will give a fluidity for scholarship quite unlikely if education is to be controlled governmentally as are roads or waterworks.

But probably the greatest change will come from all that we learned from our G.I. educational program. Recent studies show that in the higher education facilities, one half of the 2½ million students are in universities, one fourth in liberal arts colleges, and the balance are split between professional schools and junior colleges. The latter, a new part of the system, already claim an attendance of over 250,000. Our needs for great numbers of professional people show trends of more than moderate size toward governmental subsidies to individuals. The exchange students, the Fulbright plan of fellowship supported by the government, will be expanded and converted into a universal national General Education Program. This G.E. —instead of G.I.—program will operate between government and pupil so that the government will not enter directly into control of education. The divorce of State and Education is as important in this sense as the separation of Church and State. Moreover, education must ever be of local concern and responsibility, just as religion is personal to each individual.

The reason I am sure that the G.E. plan will become part of our way of life is that we cannot afford the present waste of our greatest resource—man's ingenuity and mental capacities. Only one half of those who rank highest in high schools ever go to college. In fact one fifth of the top one half in the high schools are either not financially able, or are not allowed to finish high school.

Each qualifying student—with standards locally determined—will get his G.E. grant for college. There will be no threat, as at present, of government control of colleges and universities; a threat so real that some of the outstanding institutions have rejected proffers of government research grants, while others are in peril if the government suddenly withdraws its support. Furthermore, this type of direct personal subsidy is not objectionable in the sense of subsidies to a selected group, such as that to magazine publishers, shipbuilders, et cetera. Obviously there is a virtual identity between population and families, and between families and the student body. Only the bachelors would have a grievance, and they can more likely become parents than an average citizen could become qualified for any of our many business subsidies.

But, more important than all else, such financing will bring competition into the college business. New colleges will have to be organized for the vastly increased student body. Diversity will thrive in higher education. With the prestige values created in our leisure world, many more of our people will seek enrichment of the mind as an end in itself. Competition may come to the point where one institution will specialize in foreign languages (a few high schools today teach Russian), one will lead into social

sciences, another into the liberal arts, without concern to
pecuniary aspects of the student's later life. We will not
tend toward overspecialization. Nor in the next many
decades will we need to fear too much variety. Rather
must we be concerned with the dead levels of uniformity.
I defy any group of trained scientists to distinguish between the intellectual output of any of the dozen or so
smaller New England liberal arts colleges today.

Think of the relief that the college president will
find. His major time-consuming duty of cajoling money
out of rich alumni, big corporations and government
agencies, will be ended. He will concentrate on changes
in educational techniques. In fact, the businessman as
president may be unknown in 1976. With money supplied
by the students—instead of, as today, the students paying
only one half of cost and getting the rest as a charity—
there is some hope that educators will run education. Of
course, a scholar will have to be scholarly enough to know
his limitations. He will hire the business and executive
ability needed to prepare building programs, deal with
contractors, and manage investment portfolios. Nor will
the scholars, as trustees, find a lack of purchasable business
acumen, for by 1976 top businessmen will still seek the
prestige that comes from association with men of the
mind. Whereas today few men of learning are trustees of
colleges or members of boards of education, the wealthy
honorable executives who fill those important places in
our life do so in part because we carry on from our early
tradition the commendatory idea that education of youth

is a distinguished part of life—no matter how meagerly we pay the actual teachers.

Parental influence will lose its dominance as the student body becomes more adult. The enlarged student body will permit those colleges—faculty run—which care for education rather than for organized athletics or weekend house parties, to put the accent where they prefer; provided that, in the competition in the market of American youth they can find enough favor to reach the minimum number required for the economic survival of the college. The newer institutions will have the advantage of their own youth and smallness. By 1976 half of all present teachers will have retired. Those still at work will be naturally less pliable to new ideas than those just starting. But education of the future need not be always one generation behind. Teacher retirement will not be automatic, but in relation to the teacher's ability to keep educationally alive. Alumni of athletic prominence, and non-amateur athletics will not be needed to balance college budgets. Athletics will again be for fun and mainly intramural.

Libraries, of which we have fewer than seventeen thousand of all kinds, will be integrated with education at all levels, and new, better and traveling libraries will prosper. Delaware, Massachusetts, Rhode Island and California have close to 100 per cent population coverage; North Dakota, South Dakota, Kentucky and West Virginia about 45 per cent; and 20 per cent of our total population is without library service. Parents, for themselves and their children, will compel the spending of the few dollars needed for knowledge in covers—the enduring knowledge of mankind. It is only through books that we today know more about the world of a century ago than the people of that era knew about their own world. Long before 1976 we will provide libraries for the 27 million people in our land who today have no access to any library.

It is only during the last half century that we were possessed of enough knowledge to be aware of the need for emotional security in a child's life. Horace Mann, Froebel and Dewey were discoverers of education, even as Columbus explored the land and water of our earth. In 1976 most parents will be aware that the three R's are not the end of education, but only the starting tools. Parents are on the march, an irresistible march organized by millions, with healthy differences between battalions, with no generals in sight, but with the persistent urgency of people who feel deeply about the precious part of living —their children. They will make for our Republic a new world, despite those who are afraid of change because they have failed to keep faith with the march of time.

But what about the pupils? Just because we have failed as yet to find techniques for their effective mass articulation, it is fitting that they be considered separately from teachers and parents as an interested group.

Firstly, we will determine who shall be pupils and for how long. The trend, and hence the answer, seems obvious. Education will be extended through life. More emphasis on attendance at, and facilities for play schools with local parent controls of playgrounds are under way. The compulsive aspect of primary education will give way to a universal desire. Moreover, compulsory education will go through high schools, junior colleges and ultimately colleges. The pedagogues who now cry that there is waste in educating at our colleges the uneducable, do not realize how closely they are parroting those who objected to primary compulsory education in 1787. All minds and personalities will be enriched by the right kind of full-time education up to the ages of twenty or twenty-one—with education varied by competition and adapted to different personalities and different capacities. To those who declare that many people are unfit for more education, the clear future answer will be that the deficiency is in the educators and not in the people.

There is more than one group of dedicated teachers which has proven in essence all I hope for 1976. In one school, children of twelve years of age set up in type the stories told to the teacher by the seven-year-olds, to be used as reading material by the same children. Nine-year-olds learn arithmetic and bookkeeping by running the school store. In brief, learning can be and is fun. It is not remote from, but is the core of, life itself. Latin and Greek are enriching to those who study etymology when they are twelve or thirteen. Geometry is a means of discovering the height of the tallest building in town.

By 1976 close to one half of our people will, all through their adult lives, take courses by correspondence, or otherwise and effectively explore those aspects of life

and the unknown which excite their curiosities. Much of
this will coincide with job interests or the mental growth
of the children of the home. Forum debates and discus-
sions—still infantile in format—will develop so that more
light and less heat will ensue. Audiences will not seek
conflict just for conflict's sake.

Incidentally, education of the emotionally and in-
tellectually less fortunate in reformatories and prisons will
capture our imagination—not only because we are a people with a strain of evangelical nobility—but also so that
we can reduce the tax burdens of allowing the least adjusted to become increasingly more incurable.

Pupils will not be educated in our democracy of 1976
in disregard of our Due Process concept of life: that is,
there will be no segregation because of race, creed, color
or national origin. The 1954 decision of the Supreme
Court will be accepted fully. We will look back with
shame on our present record: 43 per cent as much spent
for a colored as for a white child in 1940, and still only
70 per cent as much in 1950. For other than financial
reasons, segregation, racial or religious, will be abandoned.
Even the voluntary religious Jim Crow schools will be
finished, because the majority is hurt equally with the
minority by segregation. The white Protestants are indeed
entitled to learn together with Negroes, Catholics or Jews.
We will find that the segregators are often hurt as much
as the segregated, for the root of segregation is the insecurity of the segregator, and the segregation aggravates
the insecurity.

In 1920 only 70 per cent of our population under fifteen years of age attended any school. By 1950 the figure rose to over 91 per cent. In 1920, 8 per cent of our people over twenty were attending school. In 1950 this figure more than doubled and now is over 20 per cent. Part of these increases is due to the complexities of our industrial society, creating a socio-economic extension of the period of youth. The people of least training commence work at about sixteen-eighteen, those with training enter industry after twenty years of age. Maybe comparison of standards of living between nations can be rightly gauged by length of education. In the Orient, for example, the starting age in industry and agriculture is six to twelve.

Surely in 1976 our education will tickle all minds, for each mind has at least one area which invites an excited teacher. Heretofore pupils have been brought up in a subjunctive mood. The future mood will be the subjective imperative. They have been taught, all too often, by born scholars, or by cowards who feared to risk the keener competition of other callings. Our students, from playschool through college, spend so much time learning that there is no time to understand. Work habits for the mind, not mere calisthenics, will always be of prime importance. But knowledge does not come full blown, and independence of the mind will be the pursuit of 1976 educators. The youth of our nation will be encouraged in their intuitions; their hunches will not be ridiculed. To excite the mind so that each person yearns for answers, and to have the knowledge of where and how to seek the answers, may well be the matrix of the new education.

We will see a shift from learning trades, since the trades will be taken over by push buttons which control other push buttons. Inventing machines, researching, and carrying on professions will be the "trades" of 1976. Such tradesmen will treat the liberal arts as necessary by-products. The joys of general learning, literature and languages will be the desiderata of the educated. For them education will not end with schools or colleges. People will seek learning for learning's sake, and not merely as an entrée to a job or to hang up a sheepskin. Above all, the teachers will be held once more in such high esteem as to invite the best of our minds into that most noble calling.

Our adult population now admits its own meager education, meager because it did not fit it to cope with the world of today. This admission is the starting point of progress. We will no longer coddle the dull at the expense of the alert. Variety and competition will provide the machinery for taking care of extremes as well as of those in between. The unusual child will not be distrusted, and parents will want their children to be wiser and more informed than they are. The new home, the doubled income, the time for parents to watch over education with tender care, will create more change between 1954 and 1976 than between 1854 and 1954.

Teachers will be trained in the concept of growth and change—a concept far easier to inculcate between now and 1976 than at any time in man's history. This is true because all of our environment will change at observable speed. The generation that first saw the start of the auto, radio and airplane can never have the same attitudes toward these formerly improbable developments as those which are held by the people who were born with the car in the garage, radio on the table and planes in the air. The manifestations of future growth in ways of living, in attitudes in the home and in community relations will parade before our eyes. We will accept and welcome, not resist or assault. Thus the folkway of current change all around us will make it easier than ever before in the history of man to have education rest on the continuity of life through conflict, challenge and change.

Chapter 9

THE HEALTHY BODY OF 1976

A RECENT PRESIDENTIAL MESSAGE DECLARED: "THE PROGRESS of our people toward better health has been rapid. Fifty years ago their average life span was forty-nine years—today it is sixty-eight years."

If the sole test of bodily health was living more years, our problem would, in a sense, be simple. At the time of the Constitutional Convention of 1787 the average age of all delegates was about forty, six were under thirty years of age, with Franklin, a biological sport, over eighty. The average of our Senate today is about fifty-six. The extension of life has proceeded in such a manner that old age is in itself now examined as an ailment, and so-called normal death is subjected to medical inquiry as a matter of ill health.

The present mortality tables show a male life expectancy of about sixty-five years, a female expectancy of

160

about seventy years. That women have a greater endurance is surely less rooted in the biology of the female body than in the cultural and industrial stresses of our time. By 1976 these will be so reduced that the discrepancy will narrow, for worry will be on the wane. I suspect that worry shortens one's days on earth, evidence of which is seen in the longevity of judges, clerics, fishermen and others removed from ordinary contests against other men. I venture the guess, too, that optimists and those who fight nature live longest.

Birth is our first health hazard. Miscarriages are more likely to be of male embryos; deaths at birth or in infancy are greater among males. To explain this I have accepted the theory that a male embryo survives with difficulty in the alien body of the mother, and hence it requires an extra bit of vitality to survive. During wars there appears to be an increase of the marriage of younger and more vital girls, thus accounting for the increase in male births.

In the last three or four decades childbirth mortality dipped from one hundred to twenty-nine per thousand live births, death in the first year of life from 10 per cent to 3 per cent. On the other hand, in spite of the increased knowledge of contraception, illegitimacy is increasing—between 1947 and 1950 from twelve per thousand unmarried women to fourteen—and abortions run at the rate of a million a year. I estimate that fewer than 20 per cent of the abortions are therapeutic and hence legal; the rest are the answer to the unwanted child in or out of marriage. This makes abortion, classified at times as murder, our number one health problem. In addition, 2,500 women die as the result of abortions each year, not to mention thousands more who suffer physically and psychologically from an inability to have children later when they want them. Of course these figures are guesses because all abortion is *thought* to be illegal and therefore statistics are not formally reported.

Suitable contraceptives, therefore, will be our single greatest contribution to the reduction of ill health. The bars against their use will go down. Actually, up to 1870, contraceptive advice was legal throughout the land. Then the Comstock laws banning it were pushed through Congress and state legislatures. In 1915 the courts started reinterpreting these laws, legalizing contraception to prevent any "threatened ailment of mother or child." This properly was expanded to include psychological preferences of the mother. Only in Massachusetts and Connecticut have the courts insisted on the bootlegging of contraceptives through doctors and druggists. Even in these two states condoms are lawful, as the jurists were semanticists enough to distinguish between them and pessaries, since condoms could also be used for prevention of venereal disease.

Only one large group of our citizens has opposed legalizing birth control information—the Roman Catholic Church—and its position has logically and wisely shifted over the years. From the beginning, admitted Catholics appeared at free birth-control clinics in their proportion to the population. Then around 1930 the rhythm method was accepted by the hierarchy of their church. With calendars, indicating the hoped-for sterile period, available indiscriminately to the married and unmarried, theological attacks on birth control as an invitation to sexual promiscuity were no longer valid. Recently ecclesiastics have condoned use of rhythm to prevent birth even on economic grounds. Soon, with the discovery of simple, esthetically acceptable means of birth control, we may expect to see universal and proper use of this greatest boon to family health.

Another sector of our health lies in an area accepted but quite overlooked, the use of our eyes and ears. At least ten million people need hearing aids, and eighty-five million wear eyeglasses. The former devices are of very recent invention and, as with glasses, were avoided until recently by the vain. By 1976, the improvement in glasses will be as great as the advance since 1795 when Benjamin Franklin designed the first bifocals. Contact lenses and direct eye correctives will reduce the number of spectacle users. The hearing aid will not only be accepted as a less obvious adornment than glasses, but will be so perfected that the use of batteries will be as outdated as the trumpet. The real progress, however, will appear in the testing of all children at very early ages for eye and ear infirmities. Thus the marking of young students as dullards or as feeble-minded, due only to their less than normal sight or hearing, will be abandoned; and corrections will take place to obviate the need of artificial aids, even though such aids are minuscule in size and increasingly concealed.

The totally deaf will all learn speech and lip reading and, from the acoustic engineers, will come the translation of sound into light and back into sound so that total deafness will no longer exist. Likewise there appears some hope of removing total blindness, except in cases where the organ itself has been entirely destroyed. Those born without either sight or hearing create, because of inner security and happiness, less of a psychological problem than those who lose their hearing or sight. The new social attitudes to such problems will reduce the misery and usual suspicions that creep in on those who have lost, rather than never had, these senses.

In considering run-of-the-mill illnesses, the problem from here on will be only one of cost of detection or cure. On this score we have done a meager job. Our medical care falls below that of many lands, including, for example, Switzerland, Austria or Israel. We have only one doctor for each 750 inhabitants. In Denmark and Holland, life expectancy is to sixty-nine, while with us it is slightly less.

We spend thirteen billion dollars a year for medical and dental services and goods, of which four billion go to doctors, and one and one-half billion to dentists, one and one-half billion for drugs, and one and one-half for miscellanies. As of July 1, 1953, seven and one-half million of us owed nearly a billion dollars to our doctors, dentists and hospitals. This debtor situation alone points to the need for a change, a change fast coming about. Already ninety million of us have some type of health insurance. A majority have hospital insurance, and some have surgical or medical insurance. Ninety per cent of gross hospital costs, 75 per cent of surgical and about 66 per cent of obstetrical costs were covered by insurance for half of the insured families. Without these new insurance techniques few hospitals could have continued to operate during the past decade.

In 1940, only fifteen years ago, less than 10 per cent of the population was covered by any such insurance. By 1976 we will all be covered for all health disabilities. The present confused battle over what is called socialized medicine will have ended. The only debatable issue, seldom explained to our people, is the one of independence of the doctor. He will continue to be tested in the market place by his patients, and so long as patients are free to pick their medical advisors, that profession will stay on its toes. With universal insurance we will have more medical schools, more doctors and more facilities. Today we are terribly underserviced. For example, only 159 doctors for each 100,000 people in the Northeast; 126 per 100,000 in the West; 116 in the North Central States and 92 in the South.

There are nowhere near enough hospital beds—in some states only five beds per thousand people. Often the hospital beds are controlled and parceled out to selected doctors on alleged medical standards, but as with the medical schools the undisclosed motivations are the enhancement or protection of medical incomes rather than the health of the nation. Few trade unions have been more successful than the medicos in controlling the number of competitors. Their present closed union and closed shop agreements will have to give way to the demands of more service to more people.

It's quite odd how accents on diseases shift through the decades and among groups. Stevedores who know how to blow a nose are immune from sinus, while infantile paralysis seems to have an affinity for high standards of living. Venereal disease, a former wrecker of lives, is now curable. Tuberculosis, now nearly finished, was the great curse of the early years of this century. In 1900 it was declared to be the principal cause of death. As late as 1945 it accounted for thirty-eight out of every one thousand deaths. By 1951 this figure was reduced to nineteen, and now T.B. has declined to seventh place as a cause of death. Pneumonia was number two in 1900. Since the discovery of penicillin in 1944, the pneumonia and influenza death rates were cut nearly in half. It's not easy now to believe that the third main cause of death in 1900 was diarrhea and enteritis, which now kill only nine out of 100,000 per year. Typhoid in a half century declined from 28 to 0.9 per 100,000, while diphtheria fell from 34.5 to 1.1. Bronchitis killed 42 out of every 100,000 fifty years ago—today only two. So the story goes—scarlet fever was reduced by 70 per cent and appendicitis by 53 per cent. Death from bacterial meningitis, the scourge of our children, was reduced in only ten years by antibiotics from over 50 per cent to less than 4 per cent of children afflicted.

Name any old-fashioned ailment and you will see the trend of its evaporation. Eighty per cent of epileptics can now lead normal lives with the use of electroencephalographs and drugs such as artance. Electroshock therapy cures involutional melancholia, while cretinism, an imbecility developed in fetal life, has virtually disappeared with the use of thyroid.

Over 300,000 of our people will be free from rheumatoid arthritis (to earn one billion dollars a year) as soon as cortisone and ACTH are made commercially available at a price people can afford. Cholera and malaria (which affect one seventh of the world's population) can be eradicated at an annual cost of less than twenty cents per capita. Even in other lands these miracles are seen. In the Philippines, in a test area, industrial absenteeism dropped from 33 per cent to 4 per cent when DDT was employed.

The stimulation of the war spurred many health efforts. In 1944 man discovered he could synthesize quinine, and recently we learned that man can surpass nature's drugs one thousand times with simpler chemical structures that avoid the toxic, and other injurious, reactions of natural products. Our chemists will learn many more short cuts.

But we are people of fads. Today it is cancer for which we spend 20 per cent of all medical research funds—and yet this totals only 26 million dollars for the five years ending 1951. The recorded cancer death rate rose in that period from 131 to 142 per 100,000 of the population, while heart disease remained constant, at 497 per 100,000, although only 10 per cent of medical funds were devoted to heart and circulatory ailments.

These shifting popularizations of fund raising for particular diseases have been less than salutary. As we fortuitously swing from one line of sympathy to another, a subtle but disastrous effect is seen in the compulsion of the younger scientists to go to that laboratory which has the biggest money bag. This is not necessarily in the direction of the cure most needed, nor even the one for which the young student has the deepest predilection. Moreover, orthodoxy in the medical profession has retarded progress.

But few among us would deny that all of the present important diseases will be detectable, preventable and curable by 1976. The true revolution will occur by spending more money for research now that man has acquired new tools of knowledge. Our increase of medical research funds was 800 per cent in the five years from 1945 to 1951, but by 1976 the government contribution (66 per cent of the total in 1951) of twenty-two millions will be increased many times over. This will be done as a thrifty investment, since the return in productivity alone will show up in tax returns.

Long before 1976 the private insurance companies of our nation will look with chagrin on their present disgraceful record of spending—out of their ten billion of income, less than one million for research as against eighteen million for advertising. Congress will find it politically wiser to spend at least as much on human health as on agricultural research. The latter figure in 1953 was eighty million, nearly four times as much as for human health.

While the organic chemist continues to eliminate susceptibility to many stubborn diseases, the laboratories will learn how to propagate viruses, just as they now grow bacteria. We will find an environment, external to the human body, for delving into the mystery of the virus. Viricides will open a great new chapter in medical therapy.

But without meaning to seem captious, I must predict a still greater relief for our people. Just as we will lick the moth and rust, the third great curse will bow before man. I refer to that ailment which in one Christmas week attacked thirty million of our people. This is none other than the common cold. The cold—undramatic and hence too much accepted, as was the case with hay fever—rates high as the cause of the loss of one and a half billion man days annually, at a cost of twenty-seven billion dollars in wages and business expenses, and eight million in medical care. The surrender of the common cold to our new magics will enhance our national productivity ten times more than the licking of arthritis.

As we conquer disease, the total hospital patients of one and a quarter million (15 per cent with Federal support) will decline, but only after an increase to at least two million before 1976. Again a word of caution. Over-all figures of facilities and beds must be applied not only to physical ailments but to the far more dire problem elsewhere mentioned—the illness of the mind. Not that the bridge between the two is any longer very definite. Psychosomatic medicine is on the march. What healthy minds will do to this technique I cannot say, but I trust that the impress of external suggestion will diminish as man attains the capacity to confess to himself his own infirmities, and admit the invalidity of his own major fears. Surely mothers, in 1976, will not start babies on the road of deception by kissing the spot where the baby hit his head. Sympathy and affection will always be freely demonstrated, but certainly not as a presumed remedy for a bump.

The deplorable overcrowding of hospitals and the underpaid, undertrained nurses (one nurse per two hospital beds) will not continue in the light of our doubled national income. Even the medical schools and hospitals will be run as trustees for the health of our people rather than as social clubs tainted with some of the worst features of old-fashioned trade unionism.

The geneticists, by 1976, will come into their own, and their accent will shift to reducing the inherited ills, such as nervous disability, blindness, and pernicious anemia. Even heart disease will be found to be not unrelated to one's ancestors. With sensible shoes, chiropodists will close shop, just as dentists will fade out with the new knowledge of diets. To be sure, only a third of our people go to the dentist even once a year.

Until we adjust to the new leisure life we may be called the phenobarbital people, but soon we will no longer be able to test our friends by snooping into their bathroom medicine cabinets. In this great shift, medicines may be diminished in quantity, and applied by doctors rather than dispensed at soda-water counters.

Gesundheit will be truly befitting only of a sneeze as we climb up the ladder of health to take care of our bodies in new terms, and with new ideas. One single change in social attitudes toward illness is essential and already in evidence. Society, through private or governmental groups, will seek out the ailing. This is now the practice with polio cases. That socially wise agency, the Infantile Paralysis Foundation, hunts up the afflicted, while other groups concerned with illnesses still hide behind social dogmas which compel the sufferer to ask for help, rather than having help offered. Such a shift in attitudes will come as care is no longer deemed a privilege but a right. Coupled therewith we will see an increased desire to live. Maybe the greatest killer of all is the absence of will—desire—to go on with life. Just as people die when they don't care about living, so also do people live when they want to live.

Old age itself will be the great new disease for man to meet as a challenge. And this challenge—everlastingly to face man—will place death in its more proper perspective as a neat end of a chapter, as the finish of an adventure called living, as the crossing of the tape at the end of a leisurely passage, rather than as the crashing of a barrier after an unappreciated combat.

Chapter 10

THE SOUND MIND OF 1976

ALTHOUGH MAN IS DETECTING MANY SO-CALLED NEW DIS-eases, the novelty is usually only in the detection. Probably the only area of newness in bodily ailments arises where man comes in contact with new portions of nature; for example, radioactive material, with which man has had too brief an acquaintance to develop immunities. Man's physical ailments, new or old, aside from leprosy and syphilis, have seldom produced shame. But there is another kind of ailment which has proverbially been surrounded by chagrin and guilt, with resulting concealments. Thus we can account for the long taboo on the treatment of those illnesses, generically known as mental ill health.

So long as people lived in farm areas or small hamlets, they could always take into their homes under conditions of partial or total concealment Aunt Milly who was a little "off her rocker." The village idiot roamed the streets freely without any danger of antisocial effect on the rest of the community, and always amidst an amused toleration of his harmless imbecility. Against this background of our mores, I see no way to use statistics or even census figures to compare, against present figures, the percentage of our people who, a hundred or even fifty years ago, were seriously mentally upset. But no longer can anyone question that mental illness is on the increase, and that it is a far greater burden, financially and industrially, on our society than all of the impacts of viruses, bacilli and accidents combined.

There are about 700,000 mental-health patients in our hospitals. They fill over 50 per cent of all our hospital beds. Various responsible authorities estimate that an additional 300,000 warrant immediate hospitalization. Close to 8½ million people, one out of every 18 persons in our nation, presently suffer from some form of mental illness sufficiently serious to force them to spend some part of their future lives in mental institutions. One out of every ten will need psychiatric care at some future time. As a footnote, our suicides (running in seasonal cycles) are not unrelated to our treatment of this problem, although, surprisingly, the rate in 1900 of 27 suicides per 100,000 has come down to about 11 today.

These 700,000 men, women and children live in our hospitals, on an average, eight years, at a per capita annual cost of about seven hundred dollars, and a total yearly cost of over a half billion dollars; or a total cost for the eight years of about four billion dollars—a sum equal to about one half of the total amount we spend annually on education. Our economy loses one million man years, or over three billion dollars' worth of productivity each year —a sum sufficient to purchase forty air-borne divisions, or equal to the entire sums spent by private and governmental institutions on all kinds of research.

During World War II nearly 40 per cent of the five million men rejected before induction, and 12 per cent of the fifteen million examined, were turned down for neuropsychiatric reasons, and 35 per cent of all medical discharges were on mental health grounds. These staggering and insulting figures exclude the quarter million discharged for such reasons as mental deficiency, drug addiction and homosexuality. The rejected would have manned 177 army infantry divisions, more than our entire military forces in the Pacific Theater of Operations in World War II.

Despite this frightening and undisputed record, only about three million dollars a year is spent on mental health research, whereas for prevention of hoof and mouth disease the federal government alone spent over forty million dollars in one year. In 1949, twenty-one states had no research program of any kind and New York, which spends a third of its entire operating budget on mental ill health, spent only one per cent of such budget on research *and* training. The people of New York spent about 140 million dollars on jewelry and watches and only about one and one-half million dollars on research and training for the mentally ill. California, which spends nearly thirty million dollars on mental hospitals, lays out less than $500,000 for research. The people of California spent 16 million dollars on chewing gum in 1951.

Nevertheless, even minor research expenditures have paid off in many fields, as for example, Noguchi's tracing of paresis to an infection of the brain. This, with the use of penicillin, cut New York State expenditures for paretic patients from five million in 1944 to under two and a half million in 1949, not to mention the substantial reduction in the former 25 per cent death rate of syphilis victims.

Electric shock treatment for involutional melancholia, estrogens for depression concomitants of menopause, and innumerable other advances are flowing from our under-financed mental health researches. Within a very short time and by minor financial contributions we will come to grips with schizophrenia, which fills 25 per cent of all hospital beds.

Hormones and drugs are being developed to retard and even cure mental ill health. As the physiology of the cell becomes better known and the chemical structure of cell and tissue is revealed, chemically induced mutations of cells may be possible. The future may bring us to a series of drugs that will permit deliberate remolding of a personality—mentally and physically. At that time the use of such drugs or electric processes will require strict controls by the state. The need for governmental standards can be seen from our knowledge of communist practices, where personalities of prisoners are emptied in thirty days by the sole destruction of the sense of time. Under com-

munist procedures the personality thus emptied during
the thirty-day so-called "cure" can be refilled with fabri-
cated events and attitudes pumped into the prisoner
during the next thirty days. Thus we note that most confessions in communist courts follow arrests by about
ninety days, with the following month used to restore the
personality to its former contours.

The powers of suggestion with or without hypnotism
will bring us to new cures by 1976. To accept such possibilities one need only ponder the capacity of some people
while asleep, but not while awake, to keep track of man-
made time so as to awake at the precise moment suggested
before going to sleep. The power of suggestion over another human being under hypnotism is not remote from
the wider powers of autohypnosis, uses of placebos and
psychosomatic medicine.

In brief, we are at the threshold of new cures derived
not only from research laboratories, but also from the 7,000
members of the psychiatric profession and the more than
1,200 mental-health clinics in the country (one-fourth of
which are presently privately sponsored, while three states
have none). Long before 1976 the number of craftsmen
in this field—researchers, psychiatrists, psychologists and
psychoanalysts—will reach unbelievable numbers, and the
research expenditures will run into billions of dollars a
year—a cheap investment in the light of existing societal
financial burdens created by ill health. Such trends can be
well seen if we recall that it is only fifty years since psy-

chiatry and sociology have been accepted and really applied to human beings.

Such expansion of personnel and money allocated to mental problems is an underestimate if the expense and incidence of crime are included under the heading of ill health. Even today we are removing juvenile delinquency from the category of crime, and shifting it to mental ill health caused by environment.

Crime, a peculiar attribute of too large cities, is on the increase—although larceny is most prevalent in cities of 100,000 to 250,000 population. The Pacific states have the highest rates for crimes against property, the Southern and South Central for murder, assault and attacks on persons. New England is the lowest in all categories of crime, and all our crimes against persons increase in the summer, and those against property in the winter.

Children under fifteen account for less than one per cent of all arrests; of sixteen to twenty years of age for 12 per cent; and twenty-one to twenty-five years of age for 16 per cent. Once again the figures are without precise value, since more than 50 per cent of juvenile delinquency cases are handled unofficially, a practice most prevalent among the wealthy. In general terms, crimes against property have kept pace with population or economic conditions, but crimes against persons are on the increase. The latter peculiarly stem from mental conditions created by school and home.

Sigmund Freud will be deemed to have given man a

more important clue toward his future than all the contributions of the physical scientists. That Freud's impress occurred at the start of our violent shift to a potential of increased leisure, and the concurrent loss of the stabilizing influences of the church, may be one of those fated historical coincidences of deep significance. On many important troublesome problems the churches ordered our lives. Of course this was a supreme comfort to those millions who wanted to avoid taking on the responsibilities of decision-making. Thus it is no overstatement to indicate that the mental ill health of our people (far beyond that of non-leisure cultures still bound by ancient religious dogmas) was inevitable in the interval between loss of church discipline and the development of individual capacity to make decisions and consciously accept the idea that heaven can also be found on earth. Into this complicated and socially confused social scene, Freud brought the first great technique for exploring man's ability to know, and live with himself. Unless man respects and loves himself he cannot love or respect anyone else. Unless man—now for the first time capable of mastering his own life—acknowledges his own dignity, he cannot possibly admit without utter shame and defeat those infirmities which each of us possess with varying degrees of control or repair. In any event, man can only survive as an independent maker of his own rich future on earth by using his new leisure for creative satisfactions, failing which even with Freud-tools, our asylums will remain full.

By 1976 the turn of the tide will be reached. Thereafter the number of psychiatrists, and the expenditures for research into man's inability to adjust to himself and his environment, will not need to be further increased. Cures in this field of health, as in physical illness, are always of minor importance compared to early detection. Our asylum population will start to decline by 1976, as man builds fewer dreams beyond his reach, and above all, lives his life so as to satisfy his own unique creative ego desires. The new exciting leisure will establish prestige values of unorthodoxy, the antithesis of that devastatingly competitive Jones family. In fact, by 1976 we will have murdered the Joneses—the symbol of the lazy and the crutch of the ill of mind.

Chapter 11

MAN MEETS MAN

IT IS NO SACRILEGE TO SAY "KNOW THY FELLOW MEN AND they shall make ye free." Man can live in peace with all men if man meets man. Absence spells ignorance and ignorance breeds invalid fears and false prides.

Switzerland is a joyous example of millions of people living in peace, although on the surface one would believe that the two great religious divisions, the four different languages, the three national origins and the difficulties of a trilingual parliament would long ago have split that great mountainous democracy, where there is no longer a need for the secret ballot, where babies don't cry and dogs don't chase wagons or cars.

The delight I take from Switzerland's existence amidst a troubled world comes from the fact that it proves what is possible on this earth. Language and religious var-

iations can become assets for understanding, rather than
barriers between men. What is possible for Switzerland is
possible for the rest of the world, even though we attain it
by different means and in different settings. The necessary
changes in attitudes are fast coming about, and one source
of them is travel, which will help spell peace on earth by
1976. Indeed, travel of persons, goods and ideas is the essence of world freedom.

One of the miracles of our own history is that democratic processes were established in a period when it took
six weeks in winter to travel from Salem, Massachusetts, to
Richmond, Virginia, and when, in 1787, Madison of Virginia said: "I know as little about Georga (*sic*) as I do
about Kamchatka." Since then we have gone through the
revolution of travel—and by government subsidy. Lotteries financed the canals, land grants the railroads, treasury doles our modern shipping, mail subsidies our airplanes, and free—not toll—roads our car and truck travel.
Only the early sailing clippers paid their own way.

The travel of man has been helped by the impetus
given transportation by the need to distribute goods. In
1953 we spent fifty-seven billions on transport, which uses
one tenth of all our business investments and employs one
twentieth of our labor force. By 1976 a smaller proportion
of this vast system will be used to carry goods. Relocation
of plants will make for shorter hauls. The better profits
earned by businesses which defy the myth that it is more
economical to sell to the entire nation will reduce national
distribution in favor of regional—already found in soap,

beer, et cetera—with resulting reduction in tonnage demands. We require each year per person eighteen tons of things to maintain each of us at our present living standard. Such shipments were a necessary burden on our mode of living in the days of our westward expansion. But now, as we become a more settled people, we will cut down the cost of living by locating our factories nearer to sources of supply or customers.

But of course, the travel revolution of 1976 will be in the airplane, making true the dream of Hero of Greece, who flirted with the idea of jet propulsion two thousand years ago. Yet aviation is only about half a century old. No engineers of 1900 prophesied the aviation of today. No engineer guessed that Australia would have more travel—per capita more air miles than we do. But it is well known that engineers are a gloomy folk. Few ever dreamed bravely enough to keep pace with man's unexpected inventiveness. Few were as bravely prophetic as our greatest science-fiction writer, Jules Verne (1826-1905). I should think that the odds are overwhelming that new sources of energy will be developed by 1976 to the point where they are cheap enough to warrant, in commercial terms, such increased speeds that London to New York will take two hours, and short-distance rockets will carry mail from Cleveland to Chicago. We may soon, rising vertically, with electrified instead of heated energy, take off at breakfast and arrive for dinner the night before. Our present runway airfields will be converted for vertical-rising

travel. Nuclear power plants now developed for the sub-
marine will promptly be adapted for the air machine. An
ionic engine may have ten thousand times the efficiency
of any rocket of 1955. However, as we get dispersal not
only of our cities but also of our industrial plants, speed
will become less important for personal uses or for toting
the supplies needed by our people.

Even today the greatest difficulty of air travel is not
speed but slowness. Now the mind of man is about to produce that machine which possesses supersonic speeds and
is still reducible to gentle slowness, with the consequent
elimination of the major hazard of the air.

There are some indications that gust alleviators will
be developed, and fog and ice will be conquered. The
propeller will be as outworn as the old-fashioned crank on
the automobile. Passenger service will acquire reliable
schedules and the hostesses, now symbols of night clubs,
will be soon forgotten. The safety factor, already better
than in private automobiles on our roads, will grow to a
percentage higher even than the present 99 per cent. In
1976 we will have more choice in air travel, as in all else—
for some purposes we will travel slower, for others much
faster. There is also some reason to think that, analogized
to the rain movers or rain makers, man will develop a capacity to reduce the solidity of the air, one of the greatest
resistances to speed and hence an important element of
cost. The North and South Pole areas will be used for
landing bases, while space platforms high in our ether will

be established. Pickaback personal air scooters will make their appearance, and all new post office buildings will be constructed with roof platforms as landing fields.

For the private plane I see no vast development, save only the helicopter for personal use. I say this despite the dispersal of our cities, and in part because the increased leisure, which will give an opportunity for transcontinental and international week ends, will create in our public the more satisfying cultural habits which come from living an antispeedometer existence.

In the military, possibly around 1976, the present high obsolescence of planes will have been reduced, with guided missiles for some time receiving the accent of our military ingenuity. These nonliving birds will no doubt be developed to travel faster and further than planes, making the piloted airplane for some military purposes as obsolete as the present battleship in the navy.

I am not much concerned with flights to the moon, although I am informed that the laws of physics allow us to get there. We are only short the apparatus. I can believe that some future Secretary of Research in our federal Cabinet may request the necessary ten or twenty million dollars to satisfy the pressures for headlines in the newspapers and television programs.

Railroads will improve with competition, and it is most likely that the nonperishables—lumber, gravel, cement, et cetera—will never be flown. Subsidies to trucks via freely traveled socialized roads will be reduced, and the competitive disparity between free truck roads and taxed railroads will be reappraised.

The private car will fortunately shrink in size, will be designed for functional uses rather than chrome-plated conspicuous expenditure purposes, will have engines in the rear, tubeless tires, visibility of the road, with less power, and greatly decreased cost of upkeep and propulsion energy. The latter will be quite different from gas, and it is not impossible that power may come from some fissionable material, although uranium does not look to be the likely source. Even taxis will be built for human comfort.

We will regain local control over highways. Today, road builders constitute the greatest political pressure group in America. This, together with appropriations for harbors, has done more to corrupt local communities than any other single force in the nation. For example, in Massachusetts as in other states, road money often is offered to a community which does not need a road. But the local authorities do not dare reject the state benefaction. Before 1976 state money will be offered on the basis that each community may decide by plebiscite whether to use its share for roads, hospitals, schools or other designated purposes. Citizens will regain their power to ponder, choose and decide rather than just receive and spend.

We have long known that the location of our population is determined to a great degree by freight and passenger transportation rates and public road building. The

South was long discriminated against because the railroads were owned and financed by, and managed with,
Northeastern seaboard orientation. We will increasingly
use rate controls to provide inducements for population
locations, just as we now give permission for bank locations with an eye to profitable competition. Moreover, the
cities' and states' tax-relief bribes to invite plant removals
will not continue as a vital force, since unionization will
reduce competitive wage-scale advantages for the run-
away shops, and the sole economic gap will depend on
nearness to markets and the effect of climate on cost of
living.

We will be a citizenry upon whom the influences of
foreign travel have worked. With cheap transport, millions
of us will go abroad. International exchange of athletes,
musicians, actors and men of learning will exert a constant
pressure toward understanding and peace. Our own
people will learn at least three languages in childhood, as
the Swiss do. Isolationism will be destroyed by travel.

And long before 1976 we will regain the courage befitting a strong people. No longer will we be so frightened
that any one individual is deemed so powerful that we refuse him entry as a visitor for fear he will corrupt our way
of life.

Our present extensive auto travel bespeaks curiosity,
but more often mere restlessness. We will no longer use
cars compulsively. We will travel to learn, to touch beauty
and to explore the fabulous varieties of life pursued by

man in far different climes and cultures. Out of such exchange of emotion and observation the viewer and the
viewed will derive greater understanding of the potentials
of man in his new world. We will admit that we learn
more from unlikes than from likes.

Chapter 12

RELIGION 1976—ITS FUNCTION AND ORGANIZATION

ANY CASUAL DISCUSSION OF RELIGION IS APT TO INVITE AN automatic and highly emotional reaction. No longer do we in the United States kill for our religions, but the silent attidues of the press and radio symbolize the timidity in debating religion by sects, or in criticizing any organized religion. Those who still hold firmly to a particular religious form as the key to all of life's imponderables are inclined to be overdefensive. Those who feel guilty because of a failure to live up to inherited forms show their insecurity by acrid responses.

I approach comment on future trends in the functions of religious organizations with good will to all, believers and nonbelievers. I have no personal dogmatic faith other than that life without the acceptance of the unknown, and without conflict, would be unbearable. It would be as boring as the accepted image of Heaven. On the other hand,

188

since there will always be some conflict, life would be unbearable for most people without spiritual guidance. Few are self-contained to the point of striding life in solitary fashion. And still, some of our most religious men and women have never attended a church service, and many of them worship alone. Some spell God with a double o.

A modest approach to this touchy subject is to indicate that the forms and functions of religious denominations have been no more static than all other cooperative undertakings of man. Only the church elders talk of rigid morality. However, at the time of our political separation in 1776 there occurred a scarcely recognized concomitant separation of our churches from the Church of England.

Religious liberty is supposed, according to our student history books, to have been an essential of our way of life. Although much of our earliest immigration was to avoid religious persecution, there is no evidence that the Founding Fathers in 1787 favored full and equal religious liberty for all sects. In fact, our Constitution is silent on the subject of religious freedom and the First Amendment says only that the *federal* government shall not censor religions, since that power was to remain exclusively with each state. Thus in many states religious bigotries were condoned by the governments. Only three states permitted a Catholic to hold office, and, until 1844 in New Jersey, and 1877 in New Hampshire, neither a Catholic nor a Jew could hold public office. In other states Quaker edifices were burned, or Mormons were massacred. Not until the twentieth century were atheists permitted to testify in the courts of some states.

Although the separate states did not effectively guarantee religious freedom, we did firmly adhere to the principle of separation of church and state, despite minor inroads on this thesis by tax exemption. The more recent experiment of released time from public schooling for religious instruction has developed no striking danger to the separation theory. (Some churches have had to bribe the children with lollipops to induce them to forego schooling for religious education.) In retrospect, it seems to me that we might have been more successful in removing religious bigotries if the many great proclamations on religious freedom had been accepted as future goals rather than as current ways of life. In truth, the most that was generally proclaimed was equality for all Protestant sects. Still, as our devotion to the dogma and forms of organized religion declined, our many sects "tolerated" each other with more outward grace.

Our early church history indicates that the power of the church was more vital than the power of the state in creating attitudes to face the daily exigencies of life. Churches, controlled often by the leading wealthy merchants, naturally urged salvation through sweat, and the satanic dangers of idleness. Such preaching no doubt greatly increased our national income during the first century of our Republic. But as we prospered, and adopted free public schools, the prestige of the clergy diminished. Also, as people huddled in bigger cities, the minister lost the influence that comes with personal contact. Today the more vital and effective parishes are in the rural districts and the small towns. There the church—any church, in fact all churches—fills a meaningful function in intimacy with the worshipers. The church supper has roots far more potent than the Rotary Club luncheons. Except in big cities, churches are truly social centers, filling up much of the new leisure-time of the people.

In our early days the minister's life between sermons was crowded with duties as alms gatherer and dispenser, and as psychological consultant. Today most of our generous benevolence to the aged and infirm is either subsumed by government, or is carried out from national headquarters by some semiscientific, impersonal, big-business operation. Thus, our clergymen have had to shift their operations and functions.

The statistics of church membership have never been reliable. Under a census act of 1902 a decennial tabulation was ordered. It soon proved to be quite useless and misleading. Some sects like the Eastern Orthodox counted only heads of families; the Roman Catholics included all men, women and children from the time of christening; while most Protestant bodies recorded only those who joined. The census was abandoned, and so any estimate of church membership is truly in the realm of guesswork. Almanacs indicate about 250 sects with total "claimed" membership of about seventy-five million, or approximately half of our people. Of this number about one fifth are supposed to be under fifteen years of age, and hence a conservative estimate of the agnostics, atheists and those who cling to a very personal God, runs to about two thirds of our adult population.

Schisms in churches were a great divisive force in the nineteenth century when theology and forms of worship had greater significance. But the trend of the future is clearly in the direction of mergers and consolidations. Only a score of sects today claim as many as one million members. Quakers, Jews and some other smaller groups are nonproselytizing, and the shifts among all sects from one to another are quite unimportant except for the flow from the stricter to the less strict groups. The net number of conversions from Roman Catholic to Protestant is substantial and increasing; while the assimilation of non-orthodox Jews to other sects goes on at a noticeable pace.

There is little doubt that the churches are in for trouble. Not only do they face competition for many of their previous valuable services but, whether for good or bad, even those who cherish forms of worship feel at home in many churches—a satisfaction impossible in the days of battling creeds. Most churches will in the future pursue practices of self-criticism—an improbable attitude in the days when each sect spoke with certainty about its peculiar connections with the Almighty. By 1976 no church will be able to survive if it presumes to unchurch all other churches.

The churches are rich. The value of church buildings and equipment used for services, not including schools, monasteries et cetera, amounts to close to four billion dollars. These properties, plus vast investment portfolios, belong to a membership predominantly female in both urban and rural areas. We have close to 300,000 men of the cloth—the poorest paid group in our land. In the future, contributions will be more difficult to garner. Men will less likely believe that dollars will purchase immortality, or that entrance fees are noted at the pearly gates. And because money is required to support this spiritual department of our national life, the present secrecy in regard to income and disbursements will be abandoned.

Without suggesting that the state compel accurate disclosure of church statistics, I believe that soon some national Protestant church will make clear to the public the details of its own bookkeeping, a feat which in time will smoke out those bodies which are either fudging the figures or deceiving by silence. We will then procure more reliable information about contributions made annually by church followers, total amount of tax relief granted to churches, the portfolios of investments held in the church treasuries and where the money goes. The present estimate of about one and one-half billion dollars of annual contributions is scarcely an informed guess. The pressure for disclosure is likely to come about in part because of our policy of registration of lobby activities, a policy that runs smack into those religious groups which take positions on pending legislation.

But the number of supporters or dollars tells only a small part of the story. In fact, the further falling away of active rather than nominal members which will be seen between now and 1976, will most certainly call for a change in the quality and strength of our church movement. The functions of churches which will endure in the ensuing revolution are twofold: firstly, to act as guardians for the distinction between good and bad. This guidance will rely less heavily than heretofore on the ancient symbols of Heaven and Hell; nor will the definitions of good and bad be laid down in their former immutable terms. Birth control, smoking or dancing, for example, will be appraised as personal virtues or vices unbecoming as subjects of religious morality. Much of the good and bad preached in the past was little more than societal conventions in a changing world. The threat of Hell for playing on the Sabbath no longer will have any acceptance. The shorter work week, which theoretically should allow more time for attendance at services, will in fact reduce the audience of the clergy.

The other great continuing function of organized religion is to give institutional expression for the seemingly patent idea that man shall never know everything. Even the nonreligious recognize the enormity of the unknown, whether or not it be called God. The concept of imponderability seems to be essential for the process of living, and is the core of present religion. The future will reduce the number of those who are worrying about immortality, but don't know what to do with themselves on a rainy afternoon.

All religious groups symbolizing the greatness of the

unknown will have to readjust their attitudes since the explorations of science also leave a total impress of the impossibility of discovering all about anything. Hence organized churches will concern themselves rather exclusively with the non-materialistic sectors of the unknown. Mental telepathy, precognition, the growth of intuition, the processes of introspection, reflection and awareness are some of the areas where organized religious explorations will take place. Religion has long known that psychic experience can be a healthy outlet for human emotion. Scores of trained scientists will enter religious pastures by delving into the character and source of our extrasensory powers. Coincidence is more than it seems to be and most people know it. Paranormal phenomena will be examined without timidity. The religious cures of the presumably physically sick and crippled will be reexamined by the joint efforts of science and religion.

I take it to be the great function of religion to symbolize concretely the changing concepts of good and bad and the acceptance of the unknown. This is done better by a religion separated from the state than by the state, as in Russia. In the next decades we will discern this and then, for the first time, clash in understandable terms with communist religion, recognizing it as a real religion, different from ours and inferior in spiritual content. In fact our churchmen may well lead the successful debate against communist dogma.

Not even in 1976 will all our own people have learned

that the human life of each individual is sacred. But more of us will be in touch with nature and the unknown in ways that cannot fail to produce humility before the unseen. This may reduce church attendance, while supplanting the worship of dogma with our own personal appraisals of good and bad.

Recognizing this shift, clergy presently go on the radio and television, talking on subjects which would have shocked the divines of 1776. Newspaper columns and front-page pictures are sought by priests, ministers and rabbis. Understandably they endeavor to hold power by debating with nonclerics the major social and economic problems of the day. Thereby, they admit that good and bad in moral terms are no longer the sole concern of the clergy. There is scarcely a subject suitable for legislation that does not evoke the talking interest of some minister. On some subjects churches, as such, take stands: birth control, child labor, divorce, age of marriage, the right not to incriminate oneself, et cetera, et cetera. On many moral social issues there are keen divisions within each separate church—for example, McCarthyism as recently discussed pro and con by Catholic prelates.

As the churchmen left the pulpits for the soap boxes and the mikes, they often exerted leadership at the cost of dilution of their religious base—or at least religious base as conceived by the clergymen of 1776. Naturally we find a substantial falling off in attendance at the church when a magnetic cleric goes on radio or television. This became strikingly apparent when the Vatican issued a statement that viewing, or listening to a priest over the ether was not an excuse for staying home from church services!

The church position will further change through the increased governmental concern with the personal welfare of the people. All through our mores the churchmen will find competitors or active organized lay collaborators. Psychiatry and the new profession of marriage counseling are working with connubial problems to such an extent that a religious-psychological book club has gained marked significance. Nationwide drives for funds—for the sick and aged—have reduced the need of clergymen to originate appeals. As such infiltrations increase, the clergy will have to find new functions, and the demarcations between many sects will disappear. Most of the Protestant groups will have found a common denominator of forms of worship, and will unite into one great body of religious opinion. The membership—in the sense of dues-paying, or regular church attendance—of all sects will greatly decline. Joint use and ownership of church buildings by a group of sects will be the pattern of the next decades. The community church will be the only church in many towns. Thus will worshipers be able to finance ministers serving presently too small congregations. At the moment an informed guess would indicate that we have one cleric per parish of 200. But even this figure is realistically too large since probably 200,000 of our 285,000 churches are supported by fewer than 100 good men and women.

The change in prestige of clergy, and the diminution in membership, need not bespeak either lack of need for organized religious leadership nor failure of the clergy of 1976 to help guide the public conscience. The church buildings will be more in the nature of consolidated religious *and* social gathering places. Men of religion will still hold prestige for the moments of birth and death. There will be fewer superstitions, clergy will be psychologically trained and many will hold important governmental offices.

Probably the single greatest test of increased adjustment of religion to our leisure-world will be seen if church members will pay decently for the ministrations to the flock. By 1976 ministers may be paid as well as the schoolteachers of today—which, needless to say, is shockingly little.

In the meanwhile, interdenominational marriages will increase, even though today the incidence of divorce is at least twice as great in interfaith marriages as where people of the same faith set up the home. But all sectarian rigidities will lessen. Non-Catholics are only recently coming to recognize that there is no single Catholic position on many subjects on which anti-Catholic bigots find a presumed uniformity ordered from Rome. As these true positions are detected and appreciated, parochial schools —whether Catholic, or Jewish Yeshivas—will decline, and their present type of divisiveness in the education of our adolescents will tend to disappear.

To meet our new earthly rewards—to most unknown until recently—the churches will become important pur-veyors of earthly satisfactions for their flocks. Community churches of 1976 will own buildings to teach hobbies—a floor for music, one for weaving, one for woodworking, et cetera. Such buildings exist today. By 1976 this new church will act in cooperation with the reorganized school systems.

No matter what form these changes may take, there is one fuction which, so far as I can see, faces no im-mediate formidable competitor. Every society needs sym-bolic representations of forgiveness. Although many more people than ever before can create their own standards of virtue, and with the aid of psychiatry, chart a course between good and bad, there will be few who will not seek some agency outside of themselves to supply forgive-ness. How else can we who believe in the sacred freedom of each individual hope to convert the misguided fol-lowers of totalitarian movements? Maybe the churches will by 1976 attain greater prestige than ever before by leading us to forgive, and hence convert, the Communists, the Fascists and all others who derogate the sacredness and freedom of individual man.

Millions of our people will still want such religious leadership. Three million of us today buy four-leaf clovers each year, thus attesting to man's recognition of the un-foreseeable. But critical examination of life and its mys-teries—instead of the purchase of a rabbit's foot—will be a major occupation to be pursued in our new leisure hours. Man will be more fully religious in his intimacy with nature. Above all, he will learn to recognize himself for what he is, and not for what his internal censor permits him to think he is. He will thus be able better to reach the religious balance between Mercy and Justice.

Chapter 13

THE MARKET PLACE
OF THOUGHT

WE HAVE MADE TWO MAJOR CONTRIBUTIONS TO THE HISTORY
of government: the management of a growing population
with moving frontiers, under a federal instead of a national system; and the gradual withdrawal of government
from the control of press, speech, radio and movies. On
this second feat, history books have confused our people
by introducing the myth that our Constitution spoke up
for freedom of speech. Such was not the case. In 1787, at
the great Convention, not a single declaration was uttered
in favor of a free press. In fact, the First Amendment was
later urged out of fear that the new government might
undercut the power of the *states* to censor ideas. That
carefully phrased declaration merely said that *Congress*
shall not abridge freedom of press. This was set forth so
that there would be no lingering impression among the
voters that the states had given up any of their own power-

ful blue pencils. Hence, the minds of our people continued to be restricted by state rather than national controls, particularly on those three subjects for which man has had his most debilitating doubts—blasphemy, sedition and obscenity. God, State and Sex always worried the insecure.

As government became more secure, and religious beliefs less rigid, obscenity became our great legal concern, especially when neurotic Comstock, of the Society for the Suppression of Vice, ran his famous lobby in 1870. Up to that time traditional though changing sexual taboos had proven sufficient to curtail concepts too shocking for each decade. The obscenity laws, once enacted, were significant mainly because they widened the gap between public protestations and the actual practices of our daily living. In no nation has the gap between public morality and private virtue been so great.

It took about 130 years before our highest court reinterpreted the First Amendment to apply to the states just as it did to Congress. After 1920 we were ready for a nationwide pattern of freedom of ideas, and after that time neither the states nor Congress were allowed the absolute privilege of curtailing freedom of speech and press.

In 1787 free communication occurred through the town meeting, the soap box, and about one hundred weekly gazettes with circulations averaging one thousand copies. The theater was curtailed as being composed of traveling vagabonds, and when movies came they were treated like the theater or the circus, as a means of entertainment. Movies, as late as 1915, were deemed outside the free areas accorded to the printed word. Only in this decade are we at last approaching freedom from pre-censorship of movies—a status long attainable except for the fear of the producers who bathed in the corrupt safety of state censorship and the so-called voluntary controls of the Hays office. The latter is based on an agreement by all producers in restraint of trade in ideas for the silver screen. The standards of taste properly residing in each separate production company were merged into the lowest common denominator of all the companies. The Hays office determined the length of a kiss in film footage, and turned the industry into an obscene scramble of competitors for tastelessness.

When radio was developed around 1920 the state had to take charge, since the air channels were obviously scarcer than the number of people who wanted microphones. With a backward glance at our First Amendment, Congress made clear that neither it, nor the commission established to dispose of these limited and precious ether waves, should try to control the content of programs. Television followed the same course, but in addition it added one of the many anomalies of our zigzagged paths between freedom and censorship. Television is uncensored. Movies are still precensored by the key states. Hence, a picture may be exhibited to twenty million people in their homes via television—uncut and uncensored. Thereafter if it be shown in a single theater, an official state censor assumes the power to edit or cut it or even order its total banning. As a corollary to this inconsistency we took the position that documentary or news films were also free of state movie censorship, being analogized to the press rather than to the stage.

Man has always feared new media of information and nothing is more odd than man afraid. During German peasant wars the illiterate population passed from hand to hand Dürer etchings showing the clergy in hell. Thus did they communicate the new ideas of the era. I dare say those who were used to reading pictures on stone slabs were quite upset by the dangers of vellum and the stylus. The printing press of Gutenberg fostered the unholy fear that the masses might get ideas formerly available only to the elite. Such jealousy of the literate suffered a mighty blow when free public schooling took hold in our land, and newsprint and type became available to many.

In the past thirty years more important changes have occurred in the techniques of spreading ideas than in all man's previous history. The pipe lines to man's mind expanded with such variety and velocity as to defy any calm consideration of better or more democratic employment.

The pipe lines came to be controlled by fewer and fewer people, by groups looking for profits instead of men burning with ideals and ideas. In all media it became apparent that profits are more lush if the material is reduced from the taste and standards of the most educated to the mush which the near literate can digest. Newspapers printed less and less news. Reporting gave way to astrology columns, comic strips and fiction reprints. Pictures, lazy paths to unsubtle brains or unsubtle paths to lazy brains, took over much of the space formerly given to words. Books in cheap paper editions began to show breasts instead of legs on their jackets after a pollster noted that men were more attracted by bosoms than limbs. Radio and television became sterilized in the bottleneck of a few networks, with most programs aimed at millions instead of thousands. The excuse "we give them what they want," is all too often a rationalization of a publisher who relishes the sadistic and tawdry but shifts the blame to an insincere plea of "satisfying the public." Diversity in content decreases as the flood of words multiplies, and the plea of a difference between education and entertainment rises. Media which dish out large doses of crude brutality, however, are "educating" audiences to assume that sadism is normal.

By 1976 we will witness another revolution in the communication of ideas. Starting with the least ephemeral, books, we will abolish tariffs on paper and devise machines to print and bind an entire volume in a single operation. I hold in my hand a test book thus printed, an improvement that will cut costs materially. The accent on best sellers will be reduced as our public becomes critical as well as literate. Bookstores will be revived—first, of course, in the smaller communities. Rental libraries, now numbering over 100,000, will grow to at least half a million, economically sustained so that the author and publisher gain some financial returns from the rentals.

Books are now subsidized through the cheap postage rates to the extent of only 14 million dollars, or at 70 per cent. Magazines receive over 200 million dollars—a 400 per cent subsidy from the taxpayers. For books to have been able to survive at all against the subsidy to magazines has been quite a miracle. No longer will the subsidies discriminate against books. Books will not carry advertisements, but the present subsidies to newspapers and magazines on advertisements will be abolished.

Radio and television presumably are "free," though nothing in life is really free. In the days to come, radio and television will in part be unsponsored, and the consumer will pay—on his telephone bill or by gadgets attached to the receiving set—for what he wants to buy over the air. Such economic shifts will place books in their rightful status, competing in an honorable market for consumer favor.

We produce about twelve thousand book titles a year. Great Britain, with one third the population and one sixth the income, publishes about eighteen thousand titles. Fewer than 150 American authors make a living exclusively from book royalties on other than textbooks, and three fourths of all our books are bought now by 10 per cent of our people. This limited book market will not long continue. Soon we will make the great circle away from printing and return to mimeograph, multigraph or offset techniques. Thus, important manuscripts which appeal only to special groups of two or three thousand will be distributed in some photostatic form at less than one dollar a copy. The cheaper popular reprints will continue to educate readership, but since distribution costs through newsstands, machines, drugstores, et cetera, will continue to be very high in a nation our size, the titles thus marketed will in the main be only such as attract at least 200,000 readers. However, there are some signs that so-called heavy reading is not too heavy for our public. Gresham's law—bad money drives out good—will take effect in reverse: good books will drive out bad as we educate our people in leisure uses in our new schools. Of course I have no clear definition of good and bad, but the public of 1976 will seek mysteries of nature rather than mysteries of man's cruelty, will prefer to read of man's adjustment to man rather than man's surrender to man.

At present our government conducts a publishing business which sells tens of millions of copies of seventy thousand different pamphlets. Happily, this competition has elicited few complaints from magazine or book publishers, and as far as I can discover, evidenced only a slight trace of political party influence. By 1976 pamphleteering will be in private hands, sustainable and profitable after wise changes in the tariff, postal and other laws. Government reports will continue to be a substantial publishing venture, and will improve as research opens up new values to report to the people.

Newspapers will be rejuvenated through the weekly press. Although we have lost several thousand weekly newspapers, there is already an apparent spurt in the number and caliber of weeklies.

The circulation of big metropolitan papers will continue to fall while the suburban dailies are growing. Moreover, the cost of a newspaper plant will decline as fabulous new mechanical techniques come from the researchers. Soon it will require far less capital to start a daily. But, still more important, we already see that big city papers can't hold their readers over wide geographic areas or outside of city limits. They print news of some interest to great numbers of people instead of vital news to few people. People are not interested in parks, for example, but are deeply concerned about the park in their own neighborhood. Thus the big dailies have passed their peak of audience appeal while the small city dailies and weeklies are just starting on a new era of growth.

Boilerplating will be reduced. Men of character who cherish dreams for their home towns will own, publish and edit these important media of democracy. Chain operation will not find comfort in this field, and towns of 5,000 to 10,000 population will support competing weeklies. Journalism schools will benefit these weeklies, which should treble in number, reaching 30,000 long before 1976.

Daily papers are in a sorry mess and it would be difficult to view their future with any idea that they could, by 1976, be more inferior in service. We have fewer than 1,700 dailies. A few decades ago we had 2,600. In 1910, competition existed in 700 towns. Now fewer than 90 cities have competing dailies. In 1910 we hit our peak of one paper for every 35,000 people. But now we are back to the less favorable status of 1850—one paper for every 90,000 people. In Norway and Denmark there is one paper for every 12,000 people. Moreover, in our country fourteen newspaper owners control 25 per cent of the total circulation.

To start with, we will make it illegal to have chains of dailies, or absentee ownership. This we have done with gas and light companies, save only where proof can be offered to justify the savings of branch or chain operations. No newspaper will be allowed to own its forests and paper mill to the detriment of competitors who are without such sources of raw material. This philosophy of the market place we accepted when we declared that a railroad could not own a coal mine or an airline. In the future, editorial pages will be reborn and restored to vigor, a personal expression by editors who believe stoutly what they write and write what they believe. The syndicated material, particularly columns, will then find a new level, for they will have to compete against revitalized editorials of the publisher. Publishers will employ taste instead of printing syndicated peephole cruelties of such low indecencies that no person directly employed by the paper will dare hand in such stuff. In truth, the present abdication of the publishers to the syndicated columns will come to an end. The press associations limited to all too few— three for our entire nation—will find competition by new state press associations.

New machinery will reduce costs—a move that is long overdue. The lack of competition in printing machinery

led, as one might expect, to the same kind of stagnation of
ingenuity as we see in other industries, for example, the
shoe industry. Electronics applied to printing will further
cut costs and the composing room will be converted into a
typewriter or a tape recorder, and a camera.

Every nation of the world is concerned with the shortage of newsprint, the bullet of the cold war, the most
effective instrument for reaching the mind of man. Present world production is eleven million tons, of which we
produce 10 per cent and use 55 per cent. The shortage of
newsprint has embarrassed or even put out of business
many foreign publications in the battle against totalitarianism, while our use of paper for excessive packaging
and wrapping, if only slightly curtailed, could supply all
of the papers of free Europe and much of Asia. But as
literacy increases, newsprint will continue to be one of
man's scarcest commodities, if we are to rely only on old-
fashioned trees. The limbless tree—prestained and colored
while growing—is already in sight. Hypodermic needles
will go along with the electronic saw. The number, height,
and size of trees will be accelerated many times over and
with new genetics the growth from seed to giant will
take months as against present years. But although all this
is in view, I rather think the solution will come from
synthetics or waste products such as bagasse.

The advertising rates in newspapers will be revised
so as not to discriminate against the moderate-sized advertisers. At present the rate cards give an overwhelming
advantage to the buyer of great quantities of space. The

new principle of a decent rate structure is already imbedded in our law for commodities, but not for services such as advertising. This change alone will bring new prospects of profit to the publisher and help preserve free enterprise for millions of businesses in our local communities.

With all these high prospects, there is one formidable threat that hangs over this preferred commodity of our era. I refer to facsimile printing. That is, putting over the ether from New York, for example, an entire paper which comes out printed and rolling off the presses in any city of the nation, in no time at all, and at a cost far below that of rewrite men, editors, reporters, et cetera. The local distributor would add only a page or two of local news and advertisements. This exasperatingly cheap technique could boilerplate our entire press at a cost so low that local effort could not survive. Such facsimile papers actually flew our air waves from New York to San Francisco about a decade ago. Even if there were half a dozen, or fifty, separate owners of such devices, we would lose diversity, that essential ingredient of freedom.

I scarcely venture a suggestion as to how we will cope with this blackout evil. Maybe each state press association will have one such devilish machine. Maybe we will restrict the bulk sales of news and advertising matter as we have forbidden block booking of movies. Unless we are careful, facsimile can spell monopoly or near monopoly on ideas, and if a few mortals own the devil, even though they use it only for national and international news, we will have forsaken our great gamble that truth arises only from conflict of ideas—and many conflicts at that.

Magazines, in our culture, have taken the place of the book-reading habits of other lands. They exist through postal subsidies and the regimentation of national advertising. In our new era of unorthodoxy, the value and use of national advertising will diminish. Regional advertising will encourage regional magazines. I suggest that then there will be thousands of new specialized magazines carrying no advertisements at all, and finding small audiences that are willing to pay fully and directly for what they get, rather than indirectly when they buy advertised oil, breakfast foods, or perfume. Absence of magazine advertising will have a deep and wholesome effect. The test of favor then will be only with readers, and never confused by the judgment of advertisers. It will be an interesting shift when we start to see if our public will pay sixty cents for the present twenty-cent magazine, fifteen cents for an hour of radio, twenty cents for an hour of television and two dollars for a new hard-cover book. Long before 1976 we will look back bewildered on this present era, when a single magazine publisher got a federal subsidy of twenty million dollars for one year for one magazine. A 100 per cent subsidy of all content in all media might be justified to encourage the spread of knowledge —but who will defend a taxpayer subsidy on the advertising portion of a magazine or newspaper?

The present religious journals (estimated at 1,000) may keep their readers, but will no doubt discuss more nontheological aspects of life. The professional scientific and scholarly journals will of course expand, and the international exchange of all such gazettes will be facilitated in the mail pouches by abolishing any postage charges on sender or receiver. All the taxpayers of each free nation in the exchange groups will carry the burden, rather than let it rest on the purchasers alone.

Trade-union publications will alter greatly. There will be no need for boilerplating the news from the international union headquarters down to the paper of each local union, a process which presently sterilizes thought and ingenuity. These publications in the new era, when ownership of corporate stock is widely spread, will point the way to better business operations and economies. Schools for labor leaders will bear heavily on training of labor journalists. More than twenty years ago one labor college had special courses in the training of labor leaders as journalists.

Radio will be divorced—in ownership and management—from television. This will occur without the need for governmental mandate, because networks owning both radio and television will be unable to find top management content to handle radio when they see what seems to be more profitable—television. Not that radio will be less important than television. In fact, it will acquire new status. News, discussion, ideas, provocative debates will be the province of radio, with pocket or wrist receivers in common use, on the market. Radio will supply our traditional—though for the present, submerged—zeal for

knowledge and need for controversy. Television will become the entertainment, the movie of the home. Moreover, radio will get out from under the domination of
three or four networks. State networks will appear. The
indigenous talent and culture of our many areas will
broadcast through seasonal sporadic tie-ins with other
stations. The coal operator finds no value in a nationwide
hookup. He sells coal only in the winter, and little in the
South. Not all our ether culture will stem from tasteless
Hollywood or provincial New York City. The present
two-area concentration of power over talent will give way
to local and area enrichments paralleling the prospective
expansion of weekly newspapers. The present telephone-
rate schedule, which provides for sale of tie-in lines between stations, will be completely revised. At present the
Falmouth station has a good program. A Boston station
wants to pick it up. The program runs fifteen minutes.
But both stations discover that the telephone company
won't sell less than one hour of wire tie-line. This is one
of many present devices used to favor the big networks,
which, of course, get still cheaper rates for telephone
wires when they buy hundreds of hours each year. All
through the communication business mere quantity gets
undue preferences; new and small entities survive only
through extraordinary effort and ingenuity since the largest entities in each of the media have been favored by the
Congress.

Another hidden asset, the comparative courage of the
smaller entities, exists for area dissemination of ideas.

There are few more timid and easily scared people in our land than the heads of the biggest companies. Many of our enterprises are so big that they play safe, take no chances and are scared out of their wits if a dozen listeners file protests. Controversy is to be avoided. Literary mush is to be admired. But the smaller companies are willing to take chances while climbing up the lower rungs of the ladder.

Television will continue to make trouble for the movies but soon, after you buy a receiving set, you will pay for television, as for movies. The big day of confusion will come when the movie industry releases to television the fifteen thousand feature pictures produced in the past decades; which time may coincide with direct purchase of television by the consumer instead of the so-called gift by a sponsor.

The oddity of the present media business is that the bigger the sale the bigger the price. In most other businesses prices go down as volume increases. But with television, as millions of additional receiving sets were sold throughout the land, the price of time for sponsors went so high that only three hundred American companies can afford national television. The great urge of individual free enterprise will leave no such seemingly superior merchandising medium for long in the exclusive hands of multimillion-dollar business.

Moreover, the interlocking of the ownership of different media will be forbidden. No newspaper will be allowed to own a radio or television outlet. At one time, in a hundred of our cities the only publisher owned the only radio outlet. What price local democracy? Soon we will divorce ownership so that radio, movie, newspaper, magazine and television each will be separately owned. Press associations will no longer own newspapers, networks will no longer own radio or television stations, although a press association or network will be allowed to own one "show place" or testing outlet. In such a market, competition in ideas will once more thrive.

The movies will soon have gone through their attempt to meet TV competition by bigger, smaller or differently shaped screens. Then they will discover, as if it were a hidden treasure, that techniques cannot replace ideas and that our gregarious public will want to leave their homes to congregate socially to witness subtle acting of well-chosen words. To create a full-length movie requires large amounts of risk capital. The amount of human effort and talent is so substantial that a public attendance in the millions is needed to bail out the investors. Up to now our production companies have been outrageous economic failures. For decades our movie industry has never gotten back its investment out of our own domestic audience. The small profits we made equaled the amounts we took from foreign markets, and three quarters of that total came from the audiences of the British Empire. Hence, the movie business will increasingly be directed at the audiences of the world. This new international competition will reduce our feature films from large-scale, belt-made, extravagantly financed rat races into gay or sober, light or serious, but above all—satisfying—products.

At the moment our screen diet is predicated on an untrue theorem: "The penalty of sinning is suffering." The fallacy of such philosophy will in time become obvious even to producers. Escape need not flow only from the improbable and the unreal. The better vicarious release will derive from the portrayal of the hidden and inexplicable impulses back of man's infirmities and his struggle for contentment and inner satisfactions.

The second stage in the development of this industry is only just commencing. Movies were captured and developed by young men, short on culture but long on predatory ingenuity. Only now is the second generation of leadership coming into power. Moreover, since most of the companies have failed at least once, the bankers involved got some education, and maybe enough to know that producation deteriorates whenever the producer owns the consumer outlets—in this case movie theaters.

The live theater will be revived through the growth of local amateur groups trained or supplemented by one or more professionals. Suburbia will be the springboard for the rejuvenation of the theater. Out of innumerable local theaters more, and presently undisclosed, talent will become available. The ratio of the audience to people backstage makes this medium a comparative luxury. But much of this present extraordinary burden will be overcome by intelligent approaches to, and of the theater unions who, understandably though unwisely, met the

monopoly of the single outstanding producing enterprise
with demands for unnecessary employment as a substitute
for old age pensions and spreading the work. This same
monopoly power, by its control of bookings across the
country, forced theaters to convert into movie houses, and
prevented the building of new theaters in our biggest
cities. Theater rents in properly constructed edifices will
be a quarter the present charges (with office space built
over the theaters), and since rent takes about a third of
total box-office receipts, the cost of theater tickets will be
cut at least in half. Then once more there will be production companies of stability and endurance.

Lectures must not be overlooked—even though there
is little written about them—as an important medium of
ideas. At present I estimate that there are ten thousand
lectures a day, excluding the extracurricular lectures of
universities and colleges and clerics. Personal contact and
the prevalent practice of unrehearsed questions and answers place this medium in a preferred status for many
people and many subjects. The local-subject lecture will
thrive on the new vitality of the local press and the ability
of communities to obtain, with 1976 travel time, informed
experts from all over the world. Not even international
world-wide radio and television programs will undercut
the values in personal "give and take" of discussion with
significant informed people. I suggest that many of the
lectures of 1976 will be given by people from Asia, Africa
and the Pacific Islands. Africa, for example, the next continent to be fully opened up, will excite our minds as the

New World excited the old in the sixteenth century. Each town will have a building with several different-sized auditoria, usable without rent, as schools are to some extent today. The chances are the audiences will be smaller, on the average, as our people seek information on which to make up their own minds, rather than mere opinion dished out by others.

Music is on the march in terms of making and listening. Our two thousand concert halls collect more than sixty million dollars, and the sales of records of Beethoven's Ninth Symphony exceed one and one-half million dollars a year. Such trends may eventually convert the juke box into a machine for other than "hot" music. On the pay-as-you-go basis, radio stations will build reputations for music alone, and musicians will flourish as soon as we divorce the ownership of broadcasting from the production and sale of receiving sets, records or any collateral appliances which obviously must confuse the urges and motives of the disseminators. Then the originators will be paid in proportion to use of their songs, music, et cetera, just as authors will be rewarded if their books meet with favor in the rental libraries. The sidewalk art shows—of Nantucket and Washington Square—will mushroom in every city and hamlet. Prices will no longer be set by phony kudos standards, but on the basis of consumer tastes. Rental libraries of pictures will flourish, with traveling exhibits in specially equipped art gallery trains and buses. The present tax discriminations against all creative people and in favor of one-shot capital-gains entrepreneurs will be abandoned, and this one change will bring us closer to an Age of Pericles. Museums and art galleries will buy more modern work, abandoning the fetish that all work by the dead is better than any by the living. Skyscrapers will be used for museums, a century or a subject to a floor.

In 1787 Madison and Pinckney, more than most other delegates at the Convention, were interested in the arts and sciences. Madison proposed premiums for the creators of arts and literature; Pinckney had in mind federal seminaries for the promotion of arts and sciences. Out of such encouragements came our copyright protections. By 1976 these will be revised so the author or artist will dominate the monopoly of his product, but its nonpublication will lead to auction-block franchise at the highest rate of royalty developed at the auction.

Through UNESCO all restraints on the flow of ideas or art, and the raw materials needed for their creation, will be abandoned—the fifty-five national duties on newsprint, seventeen on newspapers and periodicals, the forty taxes on radio sets and recording instruments (up to 75 per cent of value), the taxes and duties on films. We will be well on the way to one unfrightened world by 1976.

All through history, before the existence of mass media, books were burned—China 200 B.C., Rome 12 A.D., France 1120, Italy 1497, Belgium 1535, and so on up to Russia 1917 to date, and Germany and Italy 1933 to the end of the war. The world can no longer afford the luxury, nor will it stand the indignity, of such murder of ideas.

All the enticing new techniques of communication are only techniques. They can be instruments of fun and joy and excitement—or of conformity, lackluster and dictatorship. To gain the first, we must maintain the tradition of trust in people more than in rulers, elected or otherwise.

But then comes the query: Are there to be no limits set by law and penal statutes? There are many good reasons for dispensing with government control over the market place of thought and taste. History and enduring writers on the subject teach that a suppressed opinion may actually be true—*vide* Copernicus, Bruno, Galileo. Moreover, the official opinion may contain only part of the truth, and unless confronted with other opinions the whole truth may not emerge for decades or centuries. Then again, if the official opinion possesses verity, it is likely to be held as an inflexible prejudice and eventually degenerate into a dead dogma.

Much the same can be said about conventions and tastes. What we feared yesterday would scarcely shock us today. In 1920 the one-piece bathing suit for women was deemed a moral danger. In 1922 Joyce's *Ulysses* was suppressed, only to be validated a few years later. In 1930 the U. S. Customs barred admission to Zorn etchings!

The timid—those who do not dare trust democracy to the fullest—would still prefer a safe official ukase, even though it be not the best, to a flexible diversity. They fear for the young and the disturbed. They would often reduce the literary diet of adults to the mush of the weak and immature. The law has long fumbled with the roots of this problem. But from now on, social science will supply the answers. We now know that there is no proof that any person, young or old, commits any specific anti-social deed because he has read a specific "bad" book. Causal relationship between behavior and any single influence of life is not that simple or direct.

This is not to say that ideas are impotent or that mass corruption is impossible. By 1976 social science will unravel the ways in which ideas affect the mind, and the circumstances under which corruption has a relationship to attitudes in life.

Modern psychology will soon take a new course. In the past it has all too often taught us how to manipulate people. In the future, manipulation will give way to the discovery of conditions under which human beings develop spontaneity and fully enjoy the responsibility of the freedom of making choices. Scientists have already identified the rigid authoritarian personality in our midst, whether Fascist, Klansman or Communist. The bigotry of each is bitter. By 1976 we will have learned the ways to free people from such prejudices, just as we have already learned to detect the weakness of the leg that needs a crutch. For all bigotries are crutches for the insecure, the impotent and the indecisive.

Government control of mental diets is also a crutch of

an extreme sort. Extreme, I suggest, because a filtered literary diet builds up minds and emotions calloused against life and weakened to the point of collapse when life catches up with such people. Thus the social scientists are discerning, in the studies of the communist personality in our land, capable, intellectual, verbal, non-motor youths, stemming from politically conservative homes of good income, and thriving on the crutches of impersonal hates and the joys of stealth. They can be saved, whereas in the communist lands there would be mass insanity if our degree of freedom of thought were to be permitted to come about suddenly on some bright spring day.

Soon science will educate our political leaders so that we will reach the minds of all those of the world bewildered by the communist dictators. All our agencies will then go to work with wisdom, at a cost of possibly a billion dollars a year. A billion is far less than the enemy of freedom spends to reach for the minds of allies to be made into slaves. A billion is far less than 2 per cent of our annual war budget. The cold war is the war at which we can excel with ease if we will listen to science for the oncoming years. It is a war of persuasion to freedom.

Long before 1976 we will end the frauds of today in the market place of ideas. The basic fraud lies in the anonymity of public utterances, no matter what medium is used. In a busy world, disclosure of source is of crucial importance. For whom are the pickets at the White House parading? Who finances the expensive anonymous magazines urging segregation of all Negroes? In other words, since we guarantee the rights of free speech and press, there is no need for cowardice and subterfuge other than to fool the public or to procure support from cowards.

Long before 1976 anonymity will end without any degree of censorship by governments. Already the theory of full disclosure, now enforced for selling bonds under the SEC, or to procure second-class, low-cost postage rates for magazines, is being extended to fund-raising. No content control—just essential knowledge so that the listener or reader can identify the source as one of the factors for making up his mind.

Furthermore, we are on the verge of clarifying the limits of permissible expression—usually described as the "clear and present danger" rule. By 1976 we will be convinced that if the comment is public, there is never a danger provided there is time to answer or, in the alternative, time to call the police. If speech toward an illegal end is secret, neither the clarity nor the immediacy of the danger can be appraised. We will conclude that secrecy toward an illegal end carries dangers. Thus will we preserve, by 1976, wider rights of public speech, and not confuse the privileges of brave people with the communist or fascist cowardry of secrecy. Freedom of speech implies an opportunity to make answer, but it also implies a willingness to exercise the right so as to make an answer possible.

Moreover, we will be ready to distinguish between speech of societal significance and that of a purely personal nature. For example, libel and slander have always been carved out as exceptions to all Bills of Rights. Soon we will reappraise peephole personal invasions of privacy, under the exemptions of libel. Our recent right-of-privacy statutes show our path.

Expanding freedoms in the communication of ideas will help us make our lives richer in mind, freer in emotions. We will be more honorable to our infirmities, more aware of our aptitudes. We will live with our own standards of joy or misery. Social science will help educate our mass media and also, through them, ourselves, to decent emotional joy. The gossip columns are in for a decline as our people live with their new rich creative leisure, and find less need for the empty vicarious joy of feigned intimacy with the so-called great of screen or stage.

The girl who envisions her fairy prince after seeing a dishonest movie or reading a tabloid may well, as a result, spend her days waiting for the improbable suitor. Such failures to act, to try, to venture, are probably the sorriest expressions of the impacts of the mass media.

The search for truth will make us humble before man's ignorance of why the bee is attracted to only a few colors, why the red-wing blackbird is timid and why the salmon go to death to spawn and why we humans by hurting others bruise ourselves.

Chapter 14

GOVERNMENT IN HAMLET
AND NATION

BEFORE LOOKING AT THE FUTURE OF OUR GOVERNMENT IT
is important to glance briefly at the birth of our nation.
Just as knowledge of the past requires a glance at the present, an appraisal of the future is helped by a backward
look.

The basic impulse for our union came from foreign
enemies. There was little effective cohesion right up to
the adoption of the Constitution, and such as did exist
stemmed from external pressures. Georgia joined because
of Spain, an enemy on its southern borders. Canada might
have been the fourteenth state if the roads had been better, and Rhode Island never did show up at the Constitutional Convention. The call for a new nation was a defensive pact with a slight demand for control over intercolony
commerce or relationships. The amount of intercolony

226

trade was so insignificant that the attempt of Connecticut farmers to smuggle pot cheese at Hell Gate, Manhattan, stands out as one of the few rare dramatic border incidents of the era.

Nevertheless, at one time it looked as if the Convention of 1787 might give Congress power to control all commerce, intra- as well as inter-state. Had the roads been passable and communication available, this might have been adopted. That Congress should have the power to veto state commerce legislation was deemed unworkable only because local legislation—for example in Carolina, controlling tobacco crops—would not be heard of in New York (the first capital) until after the crop had been garnered. Thus national controls would have been fruitless.

By and large, the competition of state governments has been of supreme value. We enjoy forty-eight state laboratories, each experimenting in the art of government. The complaints of those who cry for greater uniformity have happily not always been listened to. Uniformity should come about only after experimentation has reached close to the point of perfection, and in the field of government, perfection has little endurance in a world fast changing in terms of energy and the desires of man. Thus for years Wisconsin paved the way on labor legislation, Florida competed for favor by favorable tax advantages, Delaware by latitudes for corporate operations and Nevada by generous divorce statues. Not many attempts at uniform legislation have come to fruition. True, we gain more than we lose by uniform warehouse receipts, but chaos would result from uniform, or federal, divorce practices.

Ours is not a static government; it never was. No one at the Convention of 1787 dreamed of political parties, but most of the men present lived to see them introduced, and the two-party system remains one of the few factors in our political life constant despite all other changes. Sporadic local, state and national movements have often been prods to the two dominant parties, but never have destroyed the system. The scarcely noticed geographic dispersal of our Federal employes may have reduced the sporadic urge for new splinter parties. Only 10 per cent of our 2,500,000 federal employes are in the District of Columbia; 83 per cent are in the forty-eight states and 7 per cent abroad.

Another constant in our political life is fear and distrust of too much federal power. In 1787 it led to our cumbersome and often less than democratic system of checks and balances between Executive, Legislature and Judiciary. Each party when out of office is afraid of greater national power, but favors such power when in office. Thus Jefferson put through the Louisiana Purchase and Hoover gave the first great impetus, through the Reconstruction Finance Corporation, to putting our federal government in the private banking business.

In our early days, our officials were trained in government, students of the management of those activities which people wanted to conduct jointly. Also they had time to read, think and contemplate. Recently the grandeur of amateurism has been deemed sufficient to take the place of expertness. Also, in this hectic age, no cabinet officer has time to read the letters he signs or know the contents of contracts which bear his name. The President must read no less than 400,000 words a week or rely exclusively on predigested material which leaves him at the mercy of the screening prejudices of his staff.

While our national government tried to come to grips with our improbable growth, state governments had problems of their own. Their boundaries, often artificial, have required interstate treaties for use of water and other purposes. At the same time, states have been overzealous in hoarding their power over cities. This antidemocratic attitude has corrupted both—the states by excessive power, the cities by too little responsibility.

The Thirteen Colonies, visionless as to the future growth of our nation, donated their western lands to the federal government which, after a reckless, corrupt land boom, voted to the states in 1836 our only national dividend—the then fabulous amount of twenty-eight millions. As late as 1852, Daniel Webster, when opposing the development of the West by railroads, declared: "I will never vote 1 cent from the public treasury to place the Pacific Ocean 1 inch nearer to Boston than it is. What do we want with this vast worthless area—this region of savages and wild beasts, of shifting sands and whirlwinds of dust, of cactus and prairie dogs? To what use could we ever hope to put these great deserts and those endless mountain ranges?"

In our early days cities were few and small. But now the 60,000,000 people of our countryside dominate politically the 100,000,000 city folk. In Connecticut the 880,000 people in the six largest cities have so few assemblymen in the state legislature that they can be outvoted by the representatives elected by six small towns with a total population of 10,000. Los Angeles sends one state senator to speak for 4,000,000 people; one county in California with only 40,000 inhabitants also has a senator. Such is the pattern through the country.

I suggest excessive state controls as the main reason for failure to develop decent city government. A county in Maryland must go to the capital for permission to keep unspayed dogs, and Chicago must get state approval for the location of traffic lights. Mono County, California, got back from the state treasury six dollars for every one dollar it paid, while Los Angeles got back only sixty cents, and San Francisco only forty-one cents. The State of Washington doesn't believe cities have enough wisdom to license cats; Michigan still taxes the gas used by the citizens of Lansing on trucks to put out fires.

I start my picture of 1976 at the local level, for democracy must thrive first at the grass roots. We will not revert to the ideas of Plato, who thought in 380 B.C. that 5,040 was the proper population for a city. We will be nearer to Leonardo da Vinci, a vindicated dreamer, who in 1500 set forth one of our first city plans when he advocated splitting Milan's 300,000 inhabitants among ten bright and sanitary cities of 30,000 each, saying: "You will distribute the masses of humanity who live crowded together, filling the air with stench and spreading the seeds of filth and death." Without dispersal to such small cities, we will achieve by greater citizen participation many of the benefits Leonardo envisaged. The present 1,138 communities which have some form of council-manager plan will set the pattern for all cities. By 1976 there will be a school board for each school in New York, Chicago and every city which has more than six schools. There is as yet no evidence that creative personalities of past centuries were identified with big cities. We associate Goethe with Weimar, Emerson with Concord, Montaigne with his country estate, Darwin with his hatred of London, Wagner with Bayreuth, and Mendel, the Austrian monk, with a monastery garden.

Playgrounds, libraries and parks will be run by separate local committees or boards composed of people with a practical as well as a theoretical interest in each project. Funds will be supplied by the cities or states, on the basis of numbers served. Minimum standards for teachers and other local officials will be laid down for an entire borough area or county, and supplies such as pencils and books may still be purchased centrally in wholesale quantities even though there is no real saving in the purchase of supplies after a certain quantity has been bought. The saving on quantity orders is mostly a myth, and we may find that local school playground or park boards placing their own

orders will prove less costly and certainly more adventurous in the adoption of new materials. A central department of purchase cannot afford the risks of untried materials.

It takes no undue optimism to visualize the effect on
government from such participation by men and women
employing, I must add, the additional leisure hours which
will be ours. There is no sector of local government which
precludes citizen participation. Police and fire departments will be broken down into local units capable of
human management and appraisal.

I estimate that at least ten million men and women
will accept unpaid part-time positions in community work
which they can comprehend. As a corollary, more people
will join the two major political parties, accepting membership with annual dues, attending political meetings
and finally using the ultimate weapon of expression—the
ballot. Today in a hotly contested presidential election,
with no less than ten million dollars spent on radio, advertising and television, we get only 60 per cent of our
potential voters to the ballot boxes. People don't cherish
the franchise when they do not participate as an outlet of
their own concern. By 1976 participation in local affairs
will result in 80 per cent voting at national elections,
which is the British figure, and may even hit the Austral-
ian percentage of 96 per cent, which is achieved by penalties for nonvoting. In the near future the vote will be a
weapon of affirmation, and not only one of defensive veto.

Today, people over forty years of age are more inclined to have political affiliations than are those who are younger. Also, the less educated show the least degree of political adherence. With our new leisure-education many more, and younger, people will participate in active politics. The patronizing concept of the "common man" will be a misnomer of the past.

It is folly to be distressed because national polls show the factual ignorance of our people on great national and international issues. To be able to name the members of the Cabinet or discuss flexible farm subsidies or the needed number of air wings is, and will continue to be, a matter of over-all irrelevancy for most of us. Only the farmer or farm student needs to, and can be fully informed on, dairy subsidies; the fliers, on the subject of air-service appropriations. The polls looking for knowledge of local importance to people's immediate lives indicate a heartening awareness. This is as it should be; and by 1976, with millions participating in local affairs, and through innumerable taxpayer associations, leagues of voters, and the political parties, our smaller communities will be well run, experimental, and they will show the benefits of an aware, active and informed citizenry.

This general societal shift will immediately raise the prestige values of civil-service jobs. Until recently such employment carried a preferred status—permanence of employment, and old age security. Now that private employment, through legislation or trade union agreements,

affords similar or even better rewards, the civil service will
no longer peculiarly invite those who want a safe, sure,
permanent income.

Moreover, our concepts of compensation will be
stoutly revised. In government, in teaching and in certain
managerial jobs, salaries increase with length of service.
This pattern has little relation to the realities of a person's
financial burdens and responsibilities. One's greatest expenses lie in the period from say thirty to fifty years of age.
This period in many occupations will be earmarked for
top earnings, with diminution in the later years when the
children are off on their own. Maybe the federal government will edge toward such a necessary change by offer-
ing a choice for workers operating under tenure rules.
With the prolongation of life by medical science and our
untensed mood of work, this change in peaks of compensation presents no insurmountable penalties.

Other great changes in civil service will be seen.
Recording machines will reduce the stenographer's role
to one capable of performance by part-time, easily replace-
able, nonprofessional types of workers. Of course, this will
also be true of business as well as of government, and will
peculiarly affect operations such as insurance, mail-order
houses and the like. Then again, in our great governmental
rebirth, the cities, states and the federal government will
compete with industry at the colleges for the best of each
graduating class. Civil service will share the highest prestige values with researchers and professions, despite the
effort of some to deride the brain trust or egghead. Such

anti-intellectualism will be looked on with disdain. Knowledge is the best asset, and people will symbolize their esteem for ideas by placing the town hall, fire, police and other department headquarters around, but subsidiary to, the library and the school.

The big cities will be cleaner—though never as clean as smaller ones—when every home has its electric garbage disposal. Trash will be reduced as we come to see no great social value in the triple and quadruple wrappings now foisted on us by cute advertisements. The waterfronts of seaboard, river or lake will be revised as planes carry more merchandise. Then the beauties of the water edge will be once more in the eyes of the inhabitants. Congestion will be reduced with smaller, serviceable cars and more sensible buildings. The last of our skyscrapers has already been built. No one who lives above the fourth (walking distance) floor has roots in a democracy and skyscrapers for business will be recognized as economically unsound. The new cities will be planned with play space and green squares. The horror of television aerials will disappear just as did the original radio antenna.

The slums of big cities are so costly that in less than twenty years we will decide it is cheaper to raze them. No longer will slums represent 20 per cent of area, house 33 per cent of city population, and cause 45 per cent of all city service costs. Vacant lands in cities will be forced by higher taxes or induced by lower taxes into communal services—playgrounds, parking areas, et cetera. The streets will be for traffic, and not employed as free garages.

Smoke and noise—so easy to overcome—will be held in decent check by legislation or by the general ill repute cast on those who shock our ears or stench our nostrils.

We will no longer permit our city budgets to be determined by building developers. One of the major horrors of city financing results from insurance companies—free of city planning controls—erecting homes for thousands of people without concern for schools, firehouses, courts, hospitals or other essential services. City planning of homes, in this respect, will coordinate new homes to schools, libraries, and needed public utilities.

In all sectors of government, but firstly in local ones, women will become more active. Of our 307 federal judges, five are women. In other courts, about 150 women hold important posts. By 1976 women will hold far more important posts in the judicial system, elective and executive branches. The pace of this trend is seen by noting that in 1920, the first year of woman suffrage on a national basis, twenty-nine women were elected to state legislatures. By 1953 there were close to three hundred, a boost of over fifty since 1952. Ten thousand women are holding county official positions in the 3,072 counties. There is no basic sexual reason which points to disability of women for government responsibility. It may well be that just as women are the retail shoppers in our home economy, so also will they excel over men as the locally informed representatives. There are few women mayors. I suggest there will be many more in 1976, but a woman President still seems to me to be unlikely in view of the recency of woman's shift from being the chattel of her spouse.

Long before 1976 the interest in local affairs will overflow into state and federal issues and adventures. States as such, even today, do least for us functionally, and in 1976 as they relinquish power over cities they will take on a new function. Each state will become a kind of clearing house for the spread of information between local governments. The present Governors' Conference will take on official form, and will be developed more precisely by regions. Most probably states will establish regional liaisons on the basis of Federal Reserve or Judicial districts to cooperate on commercial matters. They will supervise and regulate the management of sections which are as yet too small in people or financial resources to look out for themselves. The state will clear information between schools and colleges so that competition in education will have an informed market. But states will not retain exclusively the training of teachers, as cities of moderate size will enter this field. Knowledge of city and state affairs will be increased as the local radio and television networks find an audience more aware and more excited about state problems than federal.

The decitizenship of city folk will be overcome by legislation or changes in state constitutions. Local pride, interest and knowledge will be addressed with intelligence to the vast funds presently collected by states to be turned over to local communities. Of thirteen billion dollars col-

lected by states in 1952, over four billion was distributed
to cities and local entities. Of the thirteen billion dollars
collected, over three billion came from the federal treasury.
We will see a revision of the state-city and federal-state
function of collector-dispensor. As standards of living
show less disparity between states, the function of the
national government as collector-distributor will diminish,
thus beneficially reducing some of the worst logrolled
compromises of our Congress.

Practically every state constitution needs revision. The
federal Constitution runs to about 7,500 words, but California uses 75,000 words to clutter up its basic state law.
Many state constitutions exceed 25,000 words—of frozen
confusions, and needless detail. One state has one section
of its constitution longer than the entire Constitution of our
nation. We will see complete revisions—an unfreezing process sadly needed. Texas will then be able to assimilate
the more than one hundred amendments which it has
added—a number five times as great as all the federal
amendments adopted in 165 years.

The absurd and undemocratic setup of our states has
brought about the fixation of governors' salaries (Oregon
at $1,500 per annum); legislation sessions limited to 60
days (as in Florida); creation of innumerable counties
(as the 254 in Texas); legislator pay (Rhode Island
$5.00 a day).

We will reduce the number of state legislators, now
7,234 (423 in New Hampshire alone), to an average
number small enough for deliberation. We will elect

young people to these chambers to act as catalysts for the elder statesmen who are naturally disinclined to any change. We will develop two-party systems in all states to overcome the stagnation found in one half of our states— which are one-party states. Oregon has not had a Democratic legislature since 1878. Legislatures will record and print their debates. Campaign funds will no longer determine the election returns. I suggest we will adopt the plan of Teddy Roosevelt to have the state and only the state pay campaign costs for all candidates.

Our democratic process will be implemented by many new techniques. The legislative council (adopted in Kansas twenty years ago) will be a prevalent concept. Bicameral annual legislatures will give way to unicameral biannual. The state officials will be able to concentrate on guiding, by persuasion instead of legal power, the efforts and advances occurring in varying localities. A governor will stand as a kind of spiritual leader for that quasi-artificial area known as a state. Without patronizing the localities, his annual address will point not only to the advances in the limited areas of state operation but, in terms of gracious leadership, the state message will be a report on the exciting new attitudes, experiments and plans of the cities, towns and hamlets. A governor will be a kind of intermediary between the cities on the one hand, where people live and run their affairs, and the federal government, that vast agency which no one can fully comprehend but from which stems our national pride. The federal government will ever be remote from our lives. Participation in it in day-by-day terms is practically impossible. And still it can make or break our happiness. This is the fundamental weakness of a country as big as ours. For this reason we must rely on leadership, and techniques of controls and operations far more than we need do in our towns or villages. Near our homes, even by word of mouth, we can be knowledgeable enough to make many and prompt decisions. Town meetings can reach for truth. In the national field our desires are delegated, our hopes are transferred to others, and our welfare must often be determined by a single act—one vote at an election, rather than more intimate and perpetual impacts of personal pressure on those whom we have selected to act for us.

Hence, in this significant area of government, the great changes will not arise from an over-all and totally informed body politic, nor from their prompt responses, but rather through techniques of government.

There is little that we can do about the enormousness of our federal government, other than throw back on to the states for transfer to cities as many functions and operations as possible. As our local governments become better organized by the participation of millions of people, the federal agencies will be in a better position to respond to the urges for decentralization. This will represent a reversal of present trends under which cities pass the buck to states, and states to the federal government. Washington will always have more than enough to do. It must manage a quarter of all our land—that is, the 455 million acres

owned by our federal government. Its two and a half
million civilian employees equal the total of all public
servants employed by cities, counties and states. Fifty
million dollars a year is presently disclosed as spent by
lobbies to influence our federal legislators. The sum spent
to persuade the executive departments is surely far in
excess of that. The 435 congressmen are for most of our
districts mere symbols of a fictitious democracy. Congressmen are often so remote from their constituents that when
defeated they do not go back home. Yet somehow, this odd
machinery seems to satisfy our myth of representative
government. Our citizens now have only a vague idea of
the purpose or content of the 2,500 bills and resolutions
acted on annually at the capital.

Since a congressman represents approximately 400,-
000 persons, our government is representative in name
only. In 1789, in the first U. S. Congress, we had sixty-five
congressmen for four million people, or about one for each
sixty-two thousand inhabitants; which included, of course,
unfranchised women and disenfranchised Negroes, together totaling more than one half of the total inhabitants.
By 1976 we will reduce the number of members of the
House of Representatives so that its size will be cut to
about half. Functionally and in terms of democratic theory,
present representation is no longer meaningful, and therefore a cut spells no loss in personal relations and would
reduce the body to a size where it could carry on its
duties with dignity and dispatch. Once more that body
will become deliberative and invite into its membership

the best of our students of government. A move in this direction will not come about too soon because of the vested interest of those holding or wanting the jobs. But when our people take the time to look at the waste, expense and inefficiency of the present fiction of democracy in the lower house, the present trend of increasing its size will be reversed. I should note that the House may continue to be enlarged as in the past, over the next decade or so, before the above reduction becomes an inviting political issue. The sole important result of the present formula is special-interest legislation bargained off for other special appeals of another district—all quite remote from national considerations of merit.

The Senate must remain in its undemocratic form, a form which will continue to invite not compromises but swaps or logrolling. A few oil, silver, or sugar states can bargain power against the best interests of all the people. Nothing but a strong President will be able to fend off the worst of such sectional benefactions, usually negotiated at the expense of the rest of the people.

But many far-reaching changes are likely to affect our federal government. The most important of such improvements will be in the direction of more effective relationships between the President and the Congress. We will learn by 1976 that there is slight analogy between running a big corporation or labor union, and running a government bureau. The cabinet ministers will be men educated in the business of government rather than men adept in making money out of autos, running a law office, or conducting a farm. In such a world, the cabinet names will be well known to the people at the time of appointment. Members' interests and prejudices will have been publicly appraised over the years. There will be slight need for our present conflict-of-interests laws.

In such a world, the Cabinet will sit on the Senate floor, engage in debate, inform the Congress, answer questions—but have no vote. In brief, this is the plan stoutly urged since 1864 by many Presidents, and in 1912 pressed by a special plea to Congress from President Taft, who saw in such change a real hope that a President could surround himself with men of greater stature. The ineptitude, intellectual corruption, and inordinate confusions of the press conference as a means of getting an informed public will by such a change be converted into question periods in the Congress. Furthermore, as a result of such a move there will be no necessity for a cabinet minister to appear a dozen or more times before different congress-ional committees on a single proposal for legislation. Recently one official of cabinet rank was compelled to appear before sixteen different committees to discuss a plan for preservation of our national supply of rubber.

By 1976, congressional committees will no longer duplicate and overlap each other. Rules of procedure will be civilized, and the quaint clublike rules of seniority for chairmanships will give way to the most qualified getting the gravest responsibilities. That our government functions at all under the present quaint processes, speaks well for the vitality of our people.

The Cabinet will be a cabinet of advisors—but only of advisors. The present disturbing trend of the National Security Council—which has no statutory powers but is reported to have *voted* on policies—will not be continued. There will be one executive of our nation—the President— and although the Cabinet will be set up as a functioning group of advisors instead of as a group invited to "chatter" sessions, the cabinet members will nevertheless be advisors only—never voting—only supplying attitudes for the President's final decision.

The Cabinet will be divided into two parts. The major cabinet will consist of State, Treasury, Defense, Labor, Commerce, Agriculture and one new post—Research. In France, there is now a newly created Secretary of State for Scientific Research and Technical Progress. The Attorney General and the Budget Director will sit as consultants to this supreme cabinet as well as to the general operational cabinet, in which will sit the chiefs of all other important agencies. For example, the Postmaster General, heading our leading subsidy agency, has little place in the main cabinet other than as the top advisor on political patronage, the weapon used by the executive to cajole or bargain with a senator. Commerce will be divested of its newly added functions of air and maritime supervision, and the heads of these two bureaus will find places at the operational cabinet table.

The new cabinet post, Research, will be more important than any position of today, save only possibly State and Treasury. Several score research centers are operated

for our government today through the Defense Department, Atomic Energy Commission, et cetera. Every
branch of government is engaged in research. Five per
cent of Agriculture appropriations, six per cent of Federal
Security and thirty-five per cent of Atomic Energy Commission go for research. Our Public Health Service spends
about twenty million dollars through nonprofit-making
institutions. Small and big companies are employing modern science as a means of survival in the market place. All
our present efforts in this field are spread helter-skelter,
without even a clearing house of information. The Department of Research will not centralize the explorations.
Such concentration would spell defeat for all advances.
But surely the President should be apprised by one of his
ministers as to the total of research budgets, public and
private, the avenues of inquiry deserving our greatest
gambles, and the potential effects on enriching the lives of
our people. The present federal expenditures for research
of one and one-half billion dollars (including Atomic energy) will show a greater percentage increase than any
other operation save only education, which in itself requires most research, since too often we think education is
an intuitive operation of man. The President will then
have a general picture of avenues of inquiry by subject
and dollars—oil, flies, crows, cancer, cows, people.

In helping to assemble our army of millions of scientists, researchers and professional groups, this Secretary
will find that his first clashes are against the heads of
professional associations. Particularly in those fields where

the states have seen fit to create standards, in order to protect the public from charlatanry, will there have to be professional conventions every decade to reappraise need for existing standards, and particularly the preclusion of the field toward newer sciences. The medical profession has delayed the uses of psychiatry at least a half century, just as lawyers are doing their utmost to keep the courts and clients from making full use of the new disciplines of penology, psychiatry, accountancy and the blossoming social sciences.

At present we are terribly short of engineers, doctors and biochemists—in fact, of all kinds of student apprentices in the fields of research and service to the new sciences. The Secretary of Research will supply the scientific manpower budget of the nation—by crafts, by needs, by educational facilities, by training facilities and by areas. He will do no more than illumine the forces in our society so that we can see more clearly the needs, the excitements and the profound satisfactions of those who enter the researches magnificent. He will influence by persuasion and not by power. He will even watch with concern the threat of government, and the big business subtle financial domination of our educational institutions. Above all, he will declare the stake of our nation in those social sciences that deal with the attitudes and aptitudes of people toward people, and those organized units of life—family, community and government itself. The new social sciences will thus come to prestige parity with physics and the older disciplines.

The Secretary will not spend the appropriations for direct research. Nor, I trust, will our federal government dominate the universities by holding the purse strings.

Much of the ignorance of our public about our federal government is due to the inevitable burdens we have laid on our cabinet ministers. Hence, the management of departments will be divided not by dual cabinet officials for each department, as presently proposed, but by a cabinet secretary, a congressional undersecretary and a managing undersecretary. Much progress of an unrecognized type is going on in this direction. When it is avowed and fully developed, cabinet ministers will once more have time to think. Our Cabinet will no longer be exclusively bogged down in the problems of supervising thousands of employees, devising budgets and educating the public, but rather will become a corps of glimpsers of the future.

Since our economy will be subjected to the impersonal processes of the new energies, and the magic of electronics, the government attitudes toward commerce will take on new aspects. Our government will have to face its greatest challenge in the prevention of government operation of production at a time when business gets too big, when competition in the market place diminishes and when energy units replace work-hour or manpower units. These challenges will give birth to a new kind of Department of Commerce.

It will undergo a revolution as our factories become joyless electronically controlled belts. It will become a true advocate for free enterprise, and more particularly

will it become the slugger for a market place where mere
size does not gain advantages by power rather than ingenuity. On this department may depend the prevention of
statism through overbigness.

The national debt will increase, but our attitude toward the debt will have changed as soon as we publish national balance sheets showing all our assets and liabilities
(never yet done), at which time the debt will be viewed in
its proper perspective. We will see its relation to national
income and our ability to carry the interest thereon compared to national output. For example, in 1946 our debt
was at 220 per cent of our national income, yet, after a
substantial increase, was only 190 per cent of the national
income in 1952. Moreover, our federal debt is only part
of our total debt, and to the surprise of many, the private
debt, that is, what our people owe for mortgages, installment purchases, et cetera, exceeds the total of all public
debts—city, state and national. In 1976 I suggest that the
proportion of the private to the total debt will decline,
because private debts, generally speaking, have less validity vis-à-vis private assets than does the public debt to all
our public assets. Moreover, the spread of wealth via inheritance and income surtax rates will show a dispersal
of government bond holdings to the point of an approaching identity of creditors and debtors.

We will reverse the ideology of the Hoover Report—
at least those proposals which looked, on charts, as if government would be simplified. The Hoover report had a
design of misleading beauty, but did little more than put

more responsibility, power and work on those already swamped. The division of bureaus into categories of policy importance will replace the childish fetish of pretty chartism under which an already over-busy minister, such as the Secretary of Commerce, was loaded with the additional burden of supervising all our maritime problems and our civil airplanes.

We will have realized the curses of bigness, particularly in government. We will become aware of the long list of comparatively uncontroversial agencies, such as Geodetic Survey, the Mint, et cetera, which need not be imposed under a hypocritical fiction of coordination on the presently overburdened desks of ministers. Thus these comparatively non-controversial and substantially nonpolicy-making functions of government will once more flourish because their responsible heads will have time to know what they are about, and will be in a position to inform our people. Of course, the operations of most of these agencies will not be located at the capital, thus enriching our democracy by decentralization. Moreover, it will be possible to evoke the public interest in, and the participation of thousands of volunteer experts as advisors to these separate exciting bureaus.

Much of our government will be guided by *ad hoc* special committees. Membership thereon will be considered a high honor and the men and women so serving will be, financially and otherwise, independent of the Congress and departmental appropriations. Reports of such commissions will attain a dignity and objectivity so heartwarming as to drive out of the market place the political pabulum of the daily press and the inconsequential chatter of political party leaders. In time, party leadership will develop such stature that the parties will have clear positions on each current issue. Maybe we will be able to call up central as we now do for weather reports and find out a party's position on extension of travel grants, appropriations for medical research or amount proposed to find still cheaper substitutes for cutting forests to make newsprint.

The interrelation of federal, state and city governments will become less confused as the tax and spending programs are integrated. The national government fishes for taxes with a seine, the states with a hook and line, and the cities with a hairpin.

The total appropriations in billions of dollars are roughly:

Federal	70
All States	13
All Cities	17
Total	100

These sums come in the main from real-estate taxes, sales taxes, income taxes and the tariff.

As we refine our thinking to distinguish between wealth that has excessive power and all other wealth, our attitude toward income taxes will be revised. The amount of revenue presently collected from taxpayers with incomes of more than $20,000 per capita is insignificant.

In fact, if we took away every cent of income over $20,-
000, we would garner less than 20 per cent of our annual
budget. It would affect less than 400,000 taxpayers. The
justification for extremely high income surtax rates is psychological—to give solace to the less lucky. But a more
valid rationale will not come into existence until huge
piles of wealth are deprived of antisocial power in the
market place of business. Hence, as we control overbigness, we will leave in the hands of the wealthy the capacity
to generate new enterprises by risk investment—enterprises less readily financed by underwriting subscriptions
of thousands of people. Such a fundamental tax shift is
presently delayed by the owners or heads of big business,
who are responsible for the general public fear of excessive
power. On the other hand, the preferential taxes—called
capital gains—continue to induce mergers of businesses,
reducing the number of taxable entities. These two basic
structural facets in the federal government's major source
of revenue will be reappraised and altered in the direction of free enterprise.

The total handed out as subsidies to farmers, oil operators, magazine publishers, airline operators, shipping
campanies and innumerable other lobbywise potent
groups, amounts to more than six billion dollars a year.
By 1976 we will have reappraised our subsidies, including
tariff protections. We will find that most of the subsidies
have survived only because the facts underlying each of
them are kept away from our people. Why should we not
pay for a magazine, a gallon of gas or an airplane ride

just what it costs, plus a fair profit to the purveyor of the article?

I have done little more than touch on a few of the high spots of change. The federal government of course will have much to say about concentration of population and of energy. The outlying parts of our empire, Puerto Rico, Virgin Islands, et cetera, will become part of our commonwealth of states. The open ballot will be adopted in some small communities. This need of privacy in choosing the people to govern us exists only because of fear of indecent reprisals by employers, or government. The use of separate authorities, such as Bridge, Road or Port, will be continued as a device of decentralization and interstate efforts. Such devices will justify themselves as managerial entities, and will no longer be set up as a façade for a "toll" basis of paying for public facilities.

Although national political issues will be more diverse and intricate, and less within the knowledge of most of our people, general trends will be guided by referenda rather than by the taking of private polls. Vast referenda will be held, for in a few decades we will develop a kind of cohesiveness that will permit more precise division of opinion, but I doubt if we will ever have a score of votes on referenda in any one year, as is the case in Switzerland.

The supreme issue of government will involve the question of expansion of statism, not through ideological mass pressures, but through concentration of financial and industrial power.

We may grow up very quickly in the next decades.

Developing energy—the base of leisure—we may learn to use our new responsibilities. What we do with education, media of communication and travel will spur us to new visions of a good life for our own people but, equally important, a better life for all people. The problem is no longer who is my brother's keeper but who is my brother. From a political rebirth of brothership in the towns will flow the brotherhood in state, nation, and then of all the men, women and children on our planet.

Chapter 15

LAW

BECAUSE I AM SO FORTUNATE AS TO BE A PRACTICING AT-
torney, I approach this chapter with peculiar caution. In
fact, in a cursory fashion—unlawyerlike, I will be told—I
shall merely set forth a few of the many changes which
will come to pass in the near future.

I will single out those trends of our jurisprudence
which directly and intimately affect the lives of millions
of our citizens. This is not to mean that corporate law
does not touch the consumer's budgetary burdens, or that
rights of strike and lockout may not concern the working
people more than a new approach to the law of negligence
in accident cases. Recently I was delighted to hear of a
gift to study what law means to our people. The law as a
societal stabilizing instrument, in its search for truth in
the midst of conflict, scarcely crosses the minds of our
people.

Law, like religion and free speech, is necessary in

order to resolve different pressures—whether personal or organized. But the law has an additional unique function. Organized society can only operate with comfort if there be recognized standards of rights and duties, the conscience of the community expressed in law. Stability of legal mores in relation to the past and the future need not act as too great a brake on change and progress. To catch hold of the exact point where accepted postures should give way to future needs is the genius of the best that law can offer to society.

Much of what will happen by 1976 touches on either the function of the law, legal procedures or the legal profession. Functions do change, procedures require constant development and both are inevitably influenced by the outlook and training of those who administer the law: lawyers and judges.

The high function of law was impressed into our Constitution, yet of the three departments of our government it is the least understood. "Law" not only bewilders our people, but unhappily it is held in substantial disdain. Such costly ignorance must be charged to the profession of the bar which, for various reasons, acts as if the process of seeking truth must remain a dark mystery. Just as doctors write prescriptions so that the patients can't read them, so lawyers inject Latin or obsolete phrases whenever the laymen have an inkling of the legal issues in which they are involved. But, unlike the doctors, among lawyers no orderly system of dedication to public service has ever been adopted to counteract this language-client barrier.

Our people are underserviced in matters requiring exposition of their legal rights. This is true not only in connection with civil law, but even more so when liberty is at stake. Criminal law processes have been fouled up by the daily press which selects for interpretation as news only the horror story, the murder trial or the matching of wits. Progress in the defense of the indicted, as seen in the efforts of two hundred legal-aid societies, is unreported to our people, yet there is some progress, even though twenty-five state bar associations have not as yet even set up legal-aid committees.

In 1900 we had one lawyer for each seven hundred people; now only one for each nine hundred, even though there is more need than ever, since new legal rights—such as those flowing from social-security acts—affect millions who previously met a lawyer only at the time of default on an installment purchase, buying of a house, signing of a will, procuring a divorce or suing for accident damages.

The federal government spends about thirty millions, and the state governments sixty millions, on their judicial systems. In the last half century the number of lawyers grew from 115,000 to 181,000. The total income of all lawyers is more than two and one-half billion dollars.

Possibly because law had as its earliest object the defense of liberty against the ruling authority, in our democratic civilization criminal law still seems to many to be more important than civil. To be sure, freedom is more valuable than property, even though civil law touches the

lives of many more people than do all of the indictments
and trials for violation of penal statutes.

Few will deny that our criminal law process is one of
the most backward aspects of our national life. The main
and seldom discussed reason for this deplorable state of
affairs lies in our odd departure from the tradition of the
function of the state in England—from which most of our
states inherited their common law.

In England, in a criminal case, the Crown cannot win
and the Crown cannot lose. In other words, the duty of the
prosecutor is to obtain justice. Before 1976, I am confident
that such an attitude will be adopted throughout the
United States. No longer will prosecutors announce their
percentage of convictions or indictments. To win the case
will not be the district attorney's prime duty. My hope for
this shift is presently encouraged because the F.B.I. recently relegated to a position of minor importance, in its
annual reports, the statistical tabulations of its so-called
successes, and the present District Attorney of New York
County, unlike his predecessor, is approaching the British
practice.

The results of such a subtle change, though appearing
to be negligible, will carry vast implications. No longer
will forced confessions, holding arrested persons incom-
municado and other trickeries of the prosecution, be demanded by the public. I surmise that any prosecutor in
1976 who takes credit for a conviction or for his record of
indictments will be disbarred. As an inescapable corollary,

prosecutors will turn over all evidence of innocence to the attorneys for the defense. Ethics committees of bar associations naïvely represent that such is the present practice. In many nations a failure to so inform the defendant is ground for a mistrial. Such a change in the function and responsibility of a district attorney will do away with the absurd present notion: that just because a prosecutor "wins" one or two spectacular cases he is peculiarly qualified to be a mayor or a governor. A successful trial lawyer is not of necessity a good executive, nor does it follow that the lawyer who has been successful in suppressing the truth in behalf of clients is thereby peculiarly trained to unearth truth as a judge. The duty of the juridical system is to find truth and justice, rather than to achieve victory and headlines, yet the present mood of "get your guy" seeps down from prosecutor to police, and the attitude of the police to citizens and citizens to the police is highly adversary. All this will undergo a violent revolution. There are some signs pointing in this direction even today. In Dallas, the Chief of Police now reports to the F.B.I. every complaint by an arrested citizen of alleged violation of federal due process on the part of a policeman. This new look is being encouraged by the F.B.I. school for the training of local constables, from which two thousand local policemen have graduated after intensive special courses in handling civil liberty cases, and in the fair treatment of suspects.

In view of the vast amount of police brutality now existing, it is a delightful prospect to envisage a society tend-

ing toward the day when not all policemen will carry guns
or billies, and when the policeman becomes a friend of
the people rather than the oppressor of the alien and the
humble.

Despite the present movement for public defenders—
that is, government-appointed and paid lawyers to represent defendants—I don't believe that such a paradox will
be accepted by our people. For the state to hire one lawyer to prosecute and another to defend, as would then be
the case, would be a further admission of the foul concept that criminal law is a game of matching wits. With
judges trained in aiding the jury to find truth, the present
court circuses will come to an end. The indigent will continue to be represented, but by a bar conscious of its duty
to the community, and unashamed to represent alleged
perpetrators of crime. Above all, we will reach a firmer
faith in the assumption of innocence and the profound necessity of the state to prove guilt.

In our complex society, we have all performed forbidden acts. We have all been guilty of misdemeanors and of
even more serious crimes. The layman should realize that
there is no duty laid on a defendant to expose his guilt,
confess, or in any way aid the state in its prosecutions. This
construction is sound, because free men must always be on
guard against a too powerful state, and the state should not
only carry the full burden of proving guilt, but must at all
times place in the defendant's possession all evidence of
innocence that comes into its possession. Such an attitude
will also permeate the bench, so that we will no longer

suffer the disgrace of judges being honored because a jury brought in a verdict of guilty. The judge as interpreter of law perverts the law when he accepts praise, either for convictions or for acquittals, in his court. By 1976 an adoption of the promotion system of judges will create a better equipped judiciary.

There was a time when people thought that legal decisions emanated from Sinai, and that the law was always black or white. We still hear of "natural law." Fortunately, such escapist theory has no longer much vitality. There was a period when a chief justice of the United States was judged as being qualified to the extent that the decisions of that court were uttered as the unanimous sentiment of the judges. Unanimity seemed to bespeak a godlike wisdom. We now know that such pressures for unanimity often led to compromise down to the lowest common denominator of the bench, created bad law and precluded the next generation from using the dissenting opinions as springboards for growth and modification. The search for truth is one of the most intricate and difficult social operations in a democracy. There are two parts to law: finding and declaring the rules, the function of trained judges with the assistance of lawyers; and the finding of the fact under such rules. That those skilled in the rules of law should thereby be deemed to be wise weighers of facts, is quite illogical. The exploration for truth is the greatest research open to man, and we will, I am confident, continue to prefer the errors of jurors to the fortuitous, unconscious prejudices of judges, appointed or elected.

The new reporting devices of movies, radio and television are urged for all sorts of forums seeking truth. Though it may be admitted that their use increases the public amusement and possible knowledge, the offsetting injury to the truthfulness of witnesses, the ego inflation of judges and the effect on the entire courtroom atmosphere in the screening of evidence, will lead our people, after the first random use of the new gadgets, to revert to the former sobriety of the courtroom. But such court atmosphere will recognize the realities of our society. In thousands of our villages and small towns the witnesses and litigants are usually well known to most of the jurors and often even related by marriage to one or more of them. In fact, a juror—in the historic concept—was to be selected from the vicinage so as to be sure that he was acquainted with the habits, character and reputation of the litigants. It's a far cry from such sober intimacy, derived from life itself, to the pictures and stories selected by the uninformed prejudices of the editor of a paper or the owner of a broadcasting station. The effect on the minds of judges, jurors, witnesses and litigants should be the basis of the decision on court reporting. The public, if interested or if in need of judicial education, can bide its time until after the event. And this without encouraging star chamber procedures or reducing necessary and constant criticism of our judicial processes.

In such a new climate, either the press will treat the search for truth with the respect and dignity it deserves, or laws will be enacted to defer the pictures, headlines and pre-trial stories until after the verdict has been reached. The value of the freedom of the press must often be weighed against other countervailing desiderata of man. I am sure we will forego some general spread of information rather than imperil the hope of reaching truth.

Much overhauling of procedures will take place—cutting down delays, reducing costs of litigation. But especially in two important areas, one civil and one criminal, I am confident our people will see vast improvements in 1976. Then our present handling of the guilty will be unrecognizable. One million persons were found guilty of crimes in the first half of 1953, nearly 10 per cent more than in the same period of 1951. There are about 175,000 prisoners in federal and state jails. But our prisons neither reform the criminal nor protect society. Seventy per cent of convicts have been in jail before. Through the new social and psychological sciences, improved homes and better education in schools and churches, we will shift to curative treatment (including incarceration only where necessary), realizing that antisocial people require more and better therapy than those not in trouble with the law. Judges and jurors will be held strictly to the duty of weighing evidence and finding guilt or innocence, enough of a chore for any human, or group of humans. Persons specially trained in the new sciences will determine type and length of punishment, and above all, course of training and study for the criminal.

This is not so fanciful. Man's attitudes toward crime and punishment do change as he reviews his list of socially

offensive behavior. We execute about 100 persons annually
for murder or rape. In 1787 there were 107 offenses punish-
able by death, while in 1306 in England a man was ex-
ecuted for creating smoke by burning "sea cole." Our
parole and pardon boards are a meager step in the new
direction. So is the great decrease in hysterically long
sentences which usually deter jurors from convicting, and
seldom deter the next group of law violators.

Capital punishment will be abolished by 1976 by re-
peal of the laws or, more likely, by reluctance of jurors to
find guilt when it means death. For the state to kill a criminal is a confession of intellectual bankruptcy. And in case
of error, there is no remedy. It is done almost exclusively in
the case of murderers, and there is no evidence that it ever
deters anyone, since a high percentage of killings are emotional and irrational. Moreover, in other crimes, fewer
guilty will escape when we remove sadism as one of the
generating impulses back of sentences. Take as an example the very common offense of perjury. If the penalty
were only thirty days in jail, jurors—who also at times de-
viate from the truth—would more likely convict, than if a
lie spelled three years in jail.

We will also see great changes in our prison system.
Of all our jails, fewer than one quarter could be approved
even for adults. A recognition that criminals need special
and costly treatment to restore them to the society of free
men will save us millions of dollars and thousands of useful lives. Furloughs and conjugal jail visits will be routine
in 1976. The prison teachers and wardens will be the high-

est paid and most skilled part of our educational system.
The principal of a reformatory will rank as high as a college president. Surely the attempt to re-educate the most
disturbed is not inconsistent with the expansion of education for the more normal. We are even now rich enough to
do both, and find that both pay off in dollars.

A very different species of procedural reform will
touch the very top of our civil jurisprudence. At the highest level, a valuable aid to the administration of justice
will develop through prompt congressional review of all
opinions of the Supreme Court which construe or hold un-
constitutional the statutes previously enacted. At present
there is practically no acceptance by Congress of such a
duty. Thus confusion between legislative pronouncements
and judicial interpretations keep law in public disdain.
Such reappraisal will be helpful to the Court, which has
increasing trouble in the interpretation of hastily and
badly drawn statutes. It will aid Congress and act as a corrective in drafting further laws. It will help the public
through increased clarity of law. A high percentage of
dissenting opinions in the Supreme Court stem from badly
chosen words to describe less than precise concepts of
compromising congressmen.

Attention to clarity of legislation will apply equally to
all regulations of executive departments. This will take on
great importance, as it has long been apparent that during
the next decades much of the burden of the law courts
will be shifted to administrative agencies of a quasi-
judicial character. It is difficult to imagine how many more

judges in courtrooms we would have to have if our society had not adopted, for example, workmen's compensation laws, removing practically every dispute between worker and employer arising out of an accident. The total of these claims in 1953 in only one state would have resulted in over 200,000 new lawsuits.

The greatest single volume of business which now clogs our court calendars arises from non-employee accident or negligence cases. The defendants are usually covered by insurance policies, and after a short investigation, looking into the practices of the insurance companies, we will end this cause of congestion of court calendars. Full justice means prompt justice. Insurance companies represented by leaders of the bar have successfully smokescreened this issue by inspiring investigations every decade or so into the practices of a handful of inconsequential lawyers known as ambulance chasers. Our people will not continue to be fooled by such defensive moves, because they know that the lawyer chases the ambulance in part because the insurance company chases better and faster to get potential claimants to sign off for as small an amount as possible. In New York City, for example, three quarters of all the cases on the calendar arise out of accidents. A shift in the practices of the insurance companies at this time would save New York City millions of dollars. In the larger cities we would need fewer judges, an outcome not entirely to the liking of the legal profession or, I may add, to some of the political leaders. By 1976 all such accident cases will be removed from the courtroom and put into an administrative process analogous to that set up for Work-men's Compensation—this on the assumption that few people have accidents solely for the purpose of gaining some possible pecuniary benefits.

Since accident laws touch the lives of so many millions of our people, presently so miserably served, the change in the law process will reduce some of the present public ill will toward bench and bar.

Few realize the extent of another important impact of law. There are four thousand divorces every day the courts sit. Over 90 per cent of the decrees are by agreement between the parties in advance of trial and hence are uncontested. In all those cases, the actual court process is a routine matter performed by clerks with scissors and paste. Most of the operation is hypocritical and dishonest. The welfare of the children should invite all the wisdom a lawyer possesses. However, the agreement for their support, education, religious upbringing and health falls into a field of science for which lawyers in the main possess no craft or training. The law of divorce will be recognized to be in the field of marriage counselors rather than of attorneys. In all litigated marital affairs the children will be deemed the real clients of the advisors. Surely, no parent can divorce a child, no matter what a lawyer or court may declare. Divorce without offspring raises very different problems than divorce involving children of broken homes, and will be differently treated.

In all sectors where people meet law, the prime purpose of revaluing the procedures will be to reduce litigation and the need for judges and lawyers. I am confident that arbitration will replace much of the burden now on the court system. A few decades ago lawyers and judges, jealous of their prerogatives and fearful of losing business, argued that arbitration was illegal since it ousted the courts from their ultimate power. The laymen won out in that absurd debate. The courts gave in. Now we can predict a mighty transfer of all types of controversy to arbitration, to forums where lawyers are not so essential, and where technical rules of evidence can be wisely waived. By 1976 most business contracts, bills of sales, orders and even employment agreements will contain arbitration clauses binding on the parties. These agreements to arbitrate will preclude litigation unless the arbitrators act with fraud. Such forums for truth-seeking will produce a climate more inviting to good will, less expensive, more expeditious and, above all, capable of creating traditions of a constantly stabilizing effect on all human relations that touch on legal rights.

If men were angels there would be no need for law, and so in the final analysis, law, its function and procedures, will be colored by the quality, the aims and the ideas of the members of the bar. Today it is in the main considered *infra dig* for a lawyer to defend personal liberty except for certain polite crimes, such as violation of consumers' rights by monopolistic trusts. Moreover, corporate liberty evokes the services of the tops of the legal profession, for big fees of course, while defense of individual human rights is a field of law with which most

leading lawyers never have even a speaking acquaintance. This odd difference of value appraisals arises because the unorthodox are more often and more easily
pushed around by our society. Lawyers today feel guilty
by association with unorthodox clients, forgetting that they
defend principles as well as people. In 1976 the social direction toward nonconformity will cause the leaders of the
profession to recognize the high importance of the First
Amendment, Due Process, and the other enduring founda-
tions of individual liberty. Such defense will add to professional prestige. At that time leaders of the bar will be
leaders of freedom, and law schools will further the teaching of defense of human rights, even of the crackpots and
the most neurotic.

Thus long before 1976, the training of lawyers and
judges will be reoriented to our new society. In the first
place, there will be different training for lawyers who want
to be judges and for those who want to practice law. The
art of advocacy is not identic with the art of judging—
possibly even antithetical to it. To persuade is a different
process from weighing conflicting bits of persuasion. This
system of differential training, existing now in France, will
carry with it a concomitant innovation of great import.
Judges in the upper courts will be selected only from those
who have had judicial experience in the lower. We will
get better than amateurs on the higher benches. I leave
aside the question of nonpolitical selection of judges, since
political leaders are more inclined to favor the French sys-

tem of judicial promotions than are the leaders of the bar, who often, and naturally, hope to hit the judicial ladder at the top rung without the training and drudgery of the bottom rungs.

The present flurry of pressure that judges be nominated by bar associations will fade out long before 1976. Increasingly, we will trust the people of America rather than the legal experts. Increased power of lawyers over selection of judges would make the people still more remote from the bar and hence increase the seeming mystery of the law.

The future invites changes in legal education. Over the past decades we have swung from letting students see law in action to the thwarting process called "case law." But now, happily, we are moving away from that stultifying dogma. The new sciences of psychiatry (as to divorce, for example), penology (as to the criminal process), social sciences (as to most constitutional cases involving freedom of person or mind), are finding their way into the law schools and law books. It will take a few decades—for lawyers successful enough to be professors must often be men of orthodoxy and caution—to reappraise legal theories and societal pressures in the light of modern scientific tools. *Stare decisis*—the rule that some old case decided the point forever and a day—will be discarded. Prior decisions will be frankly read against the societal conditions of the time of the former decision, and will carry no more weight than the persuasion that goes with any prior utility. One of the excitements of the law is its constant growth. Man can't keep step with a changing way of life while he treats law as static.

Writings of decisions will be in English. This odd new pattern appeared in the fabulous opinion of Chief Justice Warren in the Segregation Cases, when his words were so unlawyerlike that a high school student could read and understand them as readily as could the most talmudic member of the bar. Bar associations should note that our Chief Justice was not reluctant to footnote the indebtedness of the Court to social science studies of bigotries and prejudices. Some law schools today are teaching how to write law briefs and opinions—a process which will surely in time affect even our legislators. The "Party of the first Part" is soon to die, and statutes will be understandable even to the men who frame them. Much of the delay in courts will be reduced by judges, in nonjury cases, reading opinions off the bench at the conclusion of the trial.

Instruction of future legal luminaries will have another bearing on justice as soon as our law schools realize that there are two separate geographic groups of lawyers —the small town and the big city. The latter is not interested in riparian rights, or damages when a cow crashes a neighbor's fence. The former can afford to be quite ignorant of the law of corporate public financing and reorganization. Maybe, without the overspecialization from which medicine and other professions suffer, we will have some law schools to ground all students in the law of individual rights, freedoms, obligations and duties, including maybe simple partnerships such as marriage and business, and only then proceed further, for those interested, to elucidate the complexities and contours of masses of wealth and power which operate as soulless creatures of the state, known as corporations.

Already some law schools are enriched by exchange students from those other democratic countries which live under quite different judicial codes. By 1976 the isolation of our legal thinking will be quite upset. Students from our own law colleges are starting to use their vacations to sit in British solicitors' offices. By 1976 the international flow of law students will be extensive, although still accented toward England, source of our great common law.

But the most profound effect on law in relation to our people will stem from the new uses of our leisure life, reducing envy and greed, putting man in better accord with his limitations and desires, increasing inner satisfactions and that kind of reasonableness which are the enemies of litigious impulses. Between men of good will, lawyers are necessary primarily to record facts against the shortness of human memory, and to counsel as to the meaning of legislative acts and personal rights. In our new kind of world there will be more men and women of good will; lawyers will become increasingly the constructive counselors of families and business enterprises.

As man's emotional life reaches a better accord with his recognized and admitted limitations and desires, his frustrations—a major cause of legal collision between people, and between people and their government—will de-

cline. Education for the creatively full life of our new leisure will enhance happiness and contentment and reduce
litigious impulses. In a more reasonable and reasoning climate, the glamour of the aggressive personality expressed
in courts of law will fade. Even today many lawyers feel
they have failed if they cannot reach for their clients fair
settlements of disputes short of litigation. It will take only
a little change in our use of leisure to reduce envies and
greed, leaving in their place greater inner satisfactions—
and that kind of reasonableness which is the enemy of the
income of the legal profession.

So that the reader should not think all this is only
wishful thinking, may I refer to Nantucket, Massachusetts,
where for years a pair of white gloves has been handed to
the circuit-riding judge whenever no crime has been com-
mitted or no indictment found since his last visit. The gloves
given would start a retail store. Even today thousands of
our communities, smaller ones to be sure, have only slight
need of courts, and millions of our people see no lawyer
for years on end. The standardization of leases, employment contracts and stockholders' rights will transfer
into tradition or convention innumerable disturbing items
which now clutter our jurisprudence. Clarity of judicial
opinions, and, more important, the understandability of
laws, will reduce litigation.

It would have been simple to add more specific
changes in this field, foreseeable in the next few decades.
Let no one think that the omissions bespeak indifference or
even coolness toward the high value I place on other re-

forms now in process. Even—maybe especially—for a lawyer-author, it seems fitting in the Utopia of 1976 to call attention to only a few of the new basic freedoms which point to a new professional way of life, a way of life eliciting greater wisdom for clients, greater satisfaction for lawyers and a warm-weather eye on the need of all people to become fully in tune with the beauty of Law as the necessary guide in the search for truth. We are seeing the beginnings of Preventive Law.

Chapter 16

WAR, PEACE AND THE U.N.

AT ABOUT THIS STAGE OF EXPLAINING TO FRIENDS MY UNITED
States Utopia of 1976, I am usually interrupted by a sharp
query: "But what makes you think there will be any life
left by 1976? Haven't you read about the hydrogen
bomb?" Many books have addressed themselves to such
queries and no human—author or not—is in a position to
write guarantees. The most I can do is to set forth my
hopes, the reasons for them and my best estimate of the
direction in which the growing desires and traditions of
peace will be carried on.

As I see mankind and its current nightmarish concern
with physical destruction, various trends are apparent.
First and foremost is the fact that our citizens are more
afraid of killing than of dying. This was proven by illuminating psychological studies carried on during the last
war. As part of our folkway, those whose duty it was to kill

gave very intimate personal names to bazookas, grenades, bombers and other instruments of death. Tender, unaggressive titles such as Gwendolyn or Mitzi were bestowed on the tools of destruction in an unconscious attempt to transfer the sense of guilt from the soldier to the weapon. Innumerable rifles later found on the front were brought back—unfired. Such are the appropriate manifestations of a people who long for peace—in fact, who organize for peace, at times even against the wishes of their elected leaders.

This adult desire to live in peace is not a trait of weakness or personal cowardice. In fact, the men who kill by order of dictators know, even if their rulers do not admit it publicly, that free men individually can fight better than slaves. Therefore, since a fully destructive combat is a psychological token of the intellectual bankruptcy of man, or a madness of dictators, the military strength of our Republic is needed only to reduce the foolhardiness of possible enemies.

To be sure, war can be instigated with increasing ease as battle becomes less democratic. Nevertheless, assuming that tools of total devastation are equally shared by us and the opposing force—dictatorship—the very severity of the weapon reduces the likelihood of use. All through life, when man is powerless to employ mild sanctions, an extreme power creates situations of nonuse. Extremes of penalty are often the same as no penalty. Even a banking supervisory agency which has no power other than to close a bank—with great hardship to depositors—is weakened by its excessive power. A banking board could correct evil more readily by firing a president than by closing a bank. So also the vastness of the war potential of nuclear weapons reduces its potential of employment. The new weapons are suicidal as well as murderous.

Coupled with such throttles we find, with the non-democratization of weapons of destruction, clear evidence that war is an incident of competitive industrial power. Farmers alone cannot conduct modern warfare. With new sources of energy, more of the earth's population will be industrialized. This means smaller families, the raising of standards of living, and less pressure from envy and competition. The gap between productive capacity of industrialized nations will narrow, and in that process the urge to battle for supremacy of productive power will diminish.

I write at this point only about bomb warfare, and leave within the expected absurd patterns of national behavior a wide area open for minor frays—such as in Korea. Minor I mean in terms of answer to the opening query: Will our civilization be ended by modern science and its destructive offspring? Furthermore, it now seems that war for the purpose of colonization is at an end.

The fact that there is no trace of old-fashioned imperialism visible in our land does not mean that in our abundance and youth we have abandoned a desire to sell our way of life to all other people. We are too young a nation to feel secure enough not to try to remake our friends into duplicates of us. This conceit shows up in most irritating form when Americans travel abroad. Foreign folkways—

often on the first American pilgrimage—appear to be inferior folkways. Travel will subdue this evangelical drive of
the insecure. We will learn much from the mores of other
people, a process which reduces the friction arising from
ignorance, a proverbial cause of man's use of force instead
of persuasion.

The danger of war, never residing in urges of the
masses, will only continue as it arises in the minds of dictators who govern people held in ignorance by controlled
press and radio, plus the rule of *ne exeat*—"Thou shalt not
leave." From this angle fascism and communism are identic. Either can endure only with a people held in blinkers.
However, the more numerous the population under a dictator, the more difficult it becomes to prevent the smug-
gling of ideas.

A few years ago our international policy was predicated on the theory that the danger of war called funda-
mentally for a battle of ideas. We were well on our way to
reaching the minds of the people behind the Iron Curtain.
More than on our way, if one is to believe, as I do, the testimony of our ablest experts, that the curiosity of the Russian people had been so aroused by our Voice of America,
reaching over seven million people, that Stalin could never
outlaw listening to our messages. No longer was that dictator in a position to make it a crime to listen to radio from
the free. Expensive jamming of the waves was the only
method of keeping the Russian people in ignorance. Just
because Russia does not favor a free market place of
thought, it is more conscious than we are that the interna-

tional war is to the mind of man. On this level we should welcome the cold war. It is a good war—a battle clash of ways of life—letting the better one win out.

Russia spends over six billion dollars a year in this cold war. We spend a mere hundred million, of which about a fifth has been for radio. Our failure in this great modern warfare may be charged in part to the blind belief that the craftsmen who are so adept in selling toothpaste or beer are the best equipped to explain democracy. These craftsmen, though they know the techniques of dissemination of Things, are crippled by their ignorance of the social forces in life and their zeal to overstate within the limits of the law. The advertiser of soap or gas can fool the consumers for a time. Advertising agents are brought up under the concept of *caveat emptor,* whereas in terms of ideologies and hopes of man *caveat vendor* is the only wise rule. The Communists always overstate their commodity. All the more reason why democracy can and should be sold in terms different from commodities or communism. Democracy will ride well on truth. Moreover, the temporary crippling of our selling job grew out of an ignorance of the psychology of the communist movement, and as is usual, ignorance leads to fear and fear leads to anything but valor and wisdom. In no sector of our antiwar policy have we ever been so stupidly thrifty in dollars or sparse in ingenuity.

Properly explained to our people, executive leadership will get warm support for a truly vast effort to secure peace by reaching the minds back of the Iron Curtain.

This, even though knowledge may not lead to agreement but rather toward a *modus vivendi* among those who favor dictatorships and those who believe the people should dictate their own destinies.

The importance of such a program is made imperative by the increased plans of the dictators to capture by infiltration. As against such warfare, we will adopt new techniques based on the difference of communism as a hope among those who are hungry, and communism as an intellectual escape for those from the middle classes who need the values of joining a crusade plus a sense of belonging. A great brief for peace will be written as soon as we understand our own 700,000 Americans, ages eighteen to twenty-three, who joined the Communist Party over a period of thirty years; left after three years; and usually came from conservative homes of moderate wealth. There is slight similarity between them and the Europeans and Asians who join communism as a hope for better economic conditions. We are about to grow up enough to make such a distinction. The anti-intellectualism drive of the past few years is spending itself, and our Executive and Legislative Chambers show some slight sign of conducting extensive campaigns to those under dictatorship on levels of reality rather than fear.

Out of our increasing national income we can afford and will spend vast sums for military preparedness. Universal military training, with no exemption except for extreme disability, will be adopted. The very universality compared to the draft will act as a democratic control of the machinery, relying, as a democracy should, on the grumbles and complaints of its citizens to correct administrative evils. Such service to the state will fit men, and women also, into functions for which they are best suited. The universal training will include ordinary disciplines, but also will be directed to language training, study of foreign folkways, development of mechanical skills and, above all, an opportunity for group behavior and leadership. Even though courage and sacrifice are more easily evoked in time of war than in peace, by 1976 we will have developed many of the moral equivalents for war. The new world of leisure and travel will be an ally of peace. But surely our greatest hope of winning by persuasion instead of by bombs lies in the experiment known as the United Nations. With us, more than with most peoples, this new device will find increased understanding and support.

The analogy to our own United States—the formation of one government out of thirteen jealous and warring colonies in 1787—will be brought home to the American people. Scarcely a problem has arisen in the U.N. since its inception that was not discussed by the Founding Fathers in Philadelphia in 1787. To give further basis for my hope, it might be well to point out that the feeble Articles of Confederation were continued for ten years before they could be reshaped into a workable Constitution. The Articles of Confederation contained no grant of *power* from the colonies and the moneys required for George Washington's army were no more than colony gifts without any penalties for nonpayment. Thus we see a parallel to the League of Nations. The year before the Philadelphia meeting, it must be recalled, Alexander Hamilton called a convention at Annapolis to form our own U.N. Only five states showed up. We did not despair. In 1787, sixty-two delegates were chosen to go to Philadelphia. Only fifty-five thought it worth their while to attend. Of the fifty-five there were only forty-two present on that last day of voting, September 15, 1787. Of the forty-two present, three would not vote for the Constitution. And still we had faith.

The document was adopted contrary to the provisions for·amendatory change contained in the existing Articles of Confederation. In most states the adoption was close, in New York by five votes and in Pennsylvania only after state police were sent out to produce a quorum of delegates at the state constitutional convention. In fact, the instrument would not have been adopted except for our first political deal—an arrangement conceived by Adams and Patrick Henry—under which the Constitution would be adopted on condition that the Bill of Rights be added by speedy amendment. Thus our own precious history teaches us that the proliferation of a constitution takes time, and only those with hope contribute anything of value.

There has already been much talk about revising the U.N. Charter so as to provide further concessions of sovereignty from the nations to the U.N. The proponents of such pressures, men of good will, have been less than persuasive because their positions have not been grounded in the history of the American people. Sovereignty is not a package deal. Sovereignty is a divisible concept consisting of innumerable units and often requires for its surrender compromises and concessions. For example, and unfortunately, our schools do not teach our children that the Founding Fathers agreed that there is one, and only one, provision in our Constitution which can *never* be amended without revolution. I refer to the provision that unanimous vote of all states is required to change the rule that each state shall have two senators. But aside from such effective undemocratic infirmity, our own Constitution distinguished with care between fields of sovereignty. Whereas immigration was to be a federal and not a state power, there was the great compromise in regard to the immigration of Negro slaves limited to a period of twenty years. The states demanded a two-thirds vote of the Senate when they gave up their sovereignty for the purpose of international treaties. However, the states demanded no such restriction in permitting the federal government to levy taxes. And as to taxes, the states waited another century and a quarter before ceding part of their exclusive sovereign right to levy income taxes.

Anyone reading the exciting minutes of the Constitutional Convention of 1787 will realize that scarcely a single final position had not been seriously discussed and at times even voted on in very different terms earlier, during the great four months of debate. For some odd reason we think that a four-year term for president, with the right to re-election, was handed down from Mt. Sinai, when in fact on many a day in the convention it looked as if the term of office might be six or more years with no right of re-election, and several delegates favored a term of fourteen years which, as was pointed out, was the median reign of a European prince.

Against these few references to the attainment of co-operative action between our states, I see signs of great hope for the expansion of the effectiveness of the U.N. without the repetition of a comparable civil war, as between our states. For example, by 1976 the question of sovereignty on the three major points of deepest concern will be resolved: the free flow throughout the planet of people, goods and ideas.

I suggest that within less than ten years, a short time in international history, a formula for selected partial surrender of sovereignty on immigration will be discussed and approved in the U.N. Obviously this country will not leave to the U.N. under its present structure and voting machinery the controls of our immigration policy. But either within limits in numbers, percentage, or by nature of votes, the nations of the world, through the U.N., will consider the right of man to roam his earth.

As for the flow of goods, the most important commodity, of course, is that which goes to the mind of man. UNESCO, so ineptly organized, managed and publicized, and operated as if it were a group of secret autobiographers, has nevertheless made the most important documentation ever set forth in the realm of free flow of thought. Tariffs on books, restrictions on newsprint, excessive postage rates on magazines and innumerable other border burdens and restrictions will be a thing of the past in 1976. Last year our nation agreed to tear down the barrier which separated our peoples from all English-speaking peoples. We had, for all intents and purposes, an embargo on the importation of British books. The richest people on earth, we were scared of British books. This fear we have abandoned.

There are very important and striking signs of a shift in our national thinking on the flow of material goods. Some of our leading bankers and industrialists at last have realized that we can only sell for export to the extent that we are ready to buy. In the automobile field, for example, we find very persuasive arguments for a horizontal cut across the board on all our tariffs. The only alternative to such a move is that we give away our wealth rather than exchange it for foreign wealth. Interestingly enough, the concept of a horizontal cut in tariffs was first pressed by the wisest American banker. A horizontal tariff cut commends itself as soon as one realizes that a proposal to cut the tariff on any particular article will always meet plausible opposition.

We can either cut our tariffs and encourage East-West trade, or continue to give financial aid to our allies. The encouragement of full East-West trade would for the next decade run to little more than a billion dollars a year since the dictator lands are short of exportable goods. A continuation of gifts to other free nations will corrupt our relationships with friends. A generous tariff cut, on the other hand, will allow us to remain in the streams of international commerce without dislocating even temporarily more than 150,000 workmen at the time of the cut. East-West trade will open up if for no other reason than to save Japan from industrial stagnation, or from joining the communist lands. Gifts will taper off as either or both of the other choices are effected.

I should imagine that the U.N. will soon adapt itself to the same subtle but vital approaches voted at the opening of our own convention. Procedurally they will copy our rules of 1787. No delegate shall talk twice until each delegate has had a chance to speak once. And all debates (in the case of U.N.—less than all) shall be secret so that men can more readily change their minds. Our Constitution would never have eventuated if the delegates had been silly enough to believe in "open covenants openly arrived at." Covenants, like all meetings of minds on highly controversial matters, must be explored without the freezing effects of publicity. After men of good will have thrashed out a proposed covenant, then is the time for projection into the full light of day for the criticism of all people.

Furthermore, the U.N. will aid peace by disclosure as distinguished from negotiation. The U.N. will be the planetary spotlight, the global social laboratory, the intellectual bourse of our world. Disclosure as a torch or as a danger signal is a more important technique than suppression, just as the spread of knowledge is more hopeful than penal sanctions. All moves in the direction of disclosure act as instruments to fend off war. Appeals for a hearing for those who believe they have grievances are signs of great hope. The emotionally distressed impulses of nations or groups of people will be treated with all the knowledge possessed by mankind; and as with a bottle of champagne, the suppressed energies do not seem too formidable after the cork is loosened and the pop once is heard.

This dream for the United Nations is of course counter to the dream of many who wish it destroyed or impotent. But history supports my optimism. A century ago nations cooperated to support lighthouses. The Universal Postal Union has facilitated transmission of information since 1875. The International Telecommunication Union, founded in 1865 to control cable lines, has now allocated frequency channels for ninety countries and eighty thousand channels. The Benelux countries have abolished *inter se* permits for travel. The ILO in Geneva has been a meeting place for sixty-nine nations to discuss labor conditions and standards. Problems concerning food, welfare of children and scientific knowledge of production (the Truman Point Four program) are discussed daily through U.N. committees and staff, and should not be overlooked as living demonstrations of a more closely knit world.

It takes time for men of widely differing cultures, languages and standards of living to accommodate one to another with sufficient understanding to form a government. The smaller the territory, the fewer the people, the easier the task. What man is now working toward, is the biggest possible government in area and peoples—and hence and the most difficult. But to one who looks underneath the reports of the daily press—or rather looks at the slow but sure growth seldom called to our attention by the press—the U.N. is on its way. It would be a miracle if it took less than a quarter of a century for a world government to get rooted in all the nations of the world, but by 1976 the U.N. will have gone through its worst periods of trial and test. Already it has contributed to peace on several occasions and in different parts of the globe where conflagrations might have arisen. Its success in fending off wars—major and minor—will be recognized.

Chapter 17

HUMAN NATURE IN A
NEW SETTING

ALREADY I KNOW THAT MANY THINK MY UTOPIA IS INSIPID,
while others deem it brash and far too hopeful. My own
opinion is that it is not difficult to extrapolate the known
facts and figures. The difficult point of deviation must
ever lie in the fact that human nature is quite unpredicta-
ble and happily does not stay put.

Whether the national income will be 800 billion or a
trillion to be divided between 190 or 210 million people
in our land is relatively unimportant compared to speculations as to how men and women will react in a strikingly
higher standard of living economy. This last chapter,
therefore, is the matrix of my dream for our people. All
the balance known as hard facts has importance only as
people's lives are affected.

To this, I address a last chapter, knowing better than
any critical reader all those multitudinous portions of life

that have been omitted. Thousands of cards filled with tidbits that add up in my outlook to the total of our folkway will now be thrown out. Ski, skywriting, soaps, sunsets, silicate, servility, stables, soul—to jot down a few of the unused lead words listed under just one letter of the alphabet. I soon found that all my dreams could not be pressed into one volume. Ours is too varied a land and too youthful a people. Those few friends who have joined in my game of Futuring invariably wondered why I had omitted this or that. I shall not try to explain or defend the inclusions or the omissions. Let those who have contra or additional speculations make answer in their own lights.

I must confess that one vital path has been traveled only lightly in various chapters because any full consideration of its potentials would have led me into another entire volume. I refer to the United States vis-à-vis the rest of the world, our presently unsought leadership, our trade and our attitudes toward free or slave peoples and governments. I trust the reader will not begrudge me this avoidance. Indeed, he may find too little of amusement or too much of hope, in my Utopia U.S.A. 1976, to be interested in any thoughts I may have about the planet. I might add that at one time I had outlined a last chapter—"U.S.A. 1976—Rest of World 2000," and I have already turned over my outside U.S.A. notes to one of my favorite economists.

Throughout my projection of 1955 facts into 1976, in terms of leisure, energy, population, food and industry, I have considered the marvels of materialism only as tools of man, always mindful that none of the tangibles created by man are an end in themselves. The value of Things is only relative to man's need and uses thereof. What I have described can happen. What will happen will flow from the conflict of dreams; yours and mine. Although the drag on progress is the nondreamers, the conflict of Utopias is the good cold war of a free society. There are good dreams and bad dreams—bad ones such as attempts to abolish the public-school system, good ones like all those pursuits of man which provide him with greater freedom of choice. In these clashes the liberal—the nondogmatic who believes in the paradise of the imagination—will be the prime persuader. As our wealth increases and free use of leisure hours becomes our clear possession, the choices we will be able to make will increase a millionfold.

At the outset I referred to the historic debate: Can you change human nature? I don't know and I don't much care because I am sure that human behavior, human desires, human attitudes change with surprising speed to meet new environments. If my 1976 social telescope depicts a small portion of the future truth, the social climate for most of our people will be further from that of 1955 than the climate of 1955 is from 1787. Today what most people want is happiness, but in our new world the potentials of man will be better expressed in the conscious pursuit of the full rich life. The dreams of the spirit will flourish with surprising strength.

Many mortals have had the capacity for supreme happiness in any environment and long before any material modern conveniences were ever designed. Happiness is what most people want, but I doubt whether it can be planned for in detail or caught up with in a chase. Happiness is fortuitous. If you are lucky you grab it going by. I never knew a person who said, "I'm going out this afternoon to get some happiness." Happiness is good for what it is, but that is not enough for my 1976. As James Harvey Robinson indicated, we invented mind and now that we know the trick we can invent more and more mind.

Mind is not enough to govern man—even a good mind. When emotions remain immature they have a peculiar and often destructive power even over the best of minds. Thoughts as well as feelings banned from consciousness can cause havoc, and the tragedy of repression is that the suppression is seldom complete. Tragedy results often on a temporary break-through. By 1976 we will know much more about the interplay between mind and emotion.

Even now, the nighttime dreams most people can remember concern other people, loves, hates, greeds and fears rather than chrome plate, emeralds or lace. Things appear in dreams only as symbols of insecurity or needs. One of the illuminating writings of 1976 will explain the greater variety in dreams of 1976 over those of 1955. Dreams may spread horizontally rather than vertically.

Virtue will take the place of morality. So in 1976 the bringing up of children with reduced jealousy for siblings, with immunized Oedipean loves or hates, and with clean, gay attitudes toward matters sexual will become a new art.

I lay particular stress on security because its absence is the root of our major cultural problem. It leads to lazy generalizations such as "I don't like Negroes, Jews or Catholics." It creates prejudice, a form of crutch sorely needed by the emotionally infirm. Prejudice is not instinctive or inborn, but in our hot, tense, competitive life of 1955 we can understand the cartoon of the tramp at the bar saying: "I hate everybody regardless of race, creed or national origin." A people secure as to food, old age and health will have less need for using any group as a scapegoat. Signs of such a life are now evident in many small, unrushed, secure villages. Such attitudes go down from parents to children—for the children are likely to conform to the bigotries or the nonbigotries of their family and associates.

In fact, this pattern is so clear in our culture that the studies of American youth who joined the Communist Party point to that illuminating and twisted imitation by opposition that declares the rule. American communism has its psychological roots in the son's battle against a reactionary father and the girl's resistance to an overwhelming mother.

An expression of insecurity is of course visible in various forms of aggression. Personal aggression, most obvious in terms of destructive juvenile behavior and of our divorce rate, is surely related to the delinquency of the parents who failed to know that aggression seldom is needed or employed by the secure. And by secure I make no point of monetary security. The major aggressions in our culture are remote from envy or greed of human possessions. Risking the chance of being controverted by some biologists, I assume that the sexually inept—the lesbian, the male homosexual and the impotent (if there be such) —have been pushed over the line by one or both parents. In our culture of heterodox sexual behavior these departures from the main stream of our pattern of life offer many outward manifestations of the typical braggadocio of the insecure. Certainly by 1976 we will no longer defeat the purpose of the heterosexual ideals of our mores by isolating and ghettoizing these departures from our cultural norm. The first step toward such change in sexual attitudes will be the recognition of the facts. Homosexual incidence now reaches 17 per cent among males, less among females. We will reach a solution in this field only because we now know that any program must derive its validity from the factual appraisal of the quantity of the division from the norm or median patterns of behavior.

One of the toughest problems confronting our people is the necessity of facing up to facts, no matter how they jar our preconceived notions which conflict with the facts. For example, in our sexual folkway we will no longer enjoy the lazy hypocrisy of talking as if the penal laws against adultery and fornication had any *raison d'être*. We will face up to the fact that over 60 per cent of all men and nearly one half of all young women have had pre-

marital heterosexual experiences. An additional 20 per
cent of the men have had premarital prostitute relationships. Not until we admit to ourselves the actual mores
can we possibly hope to effect their changes. The sexual
compromise of the Boston Puritans seen in bundling and
other practices had more validity than the blinker life we
led until very recently. The figures I quote above are
probably on the low side and will increase. For those who
cling with desperation to the myth of a premarital vir-
ginal society, one footnote fact will supply some comfort.
A goodly per cent of those who had premarital sexual affairs married a person with whom they had lived sexually
before marriage. To those who believe as I do that a high
percentage of present divorce stems from sexual amateurism and ignorance, there will be more value in more premarital sexual experience in 1976, particularly because the
mood of the relationship will contain increased elements
of taste.

We know so little about matters sexual. The subject
has only recently left the scoldings of the pulpit to enter
the laboratory of the scientists. On no subject has more
been written, but the taboos of all cultures have deflected
attention from the targets of truth. The relation of the
sexual drive to love, marriage and the parental urge has
been beclouded by societal urges for its own perpetua-
tion, incest bans and innumerable profound unmentioned
and underground or unacknowledged motivations. Man is
just beginning to assemble odd bits of knowledge garnered
by anthropology, biology and all the social sciences. We

are not entirely sure if in human mating the affinity of like for like is more potent than the attraction of opposites. At the moment we flounder among a variety of approaches—the instinct school, psychoanalytic, et cetera. We know little about the differences between male and female hormones except that the gonad of each sex secretes the hormones of the opposite. Mice, after treatment, have evidenced mating patterns of the opposite sex. We have been unable to rate in comparative importance the drives of motherhood, thirst, hunger, sex, exploration. With hypocritical taboos pervading our society until very recently, the sexual education of children was not even primitive—for many of the primitive races develop nonviolent absorptions of knowledge, nonsudden shifts to adolescence and above all, stable sex relationships.

We are now paying the price of past repressive attitudes and more particularly of religious prohibitions. The reduction of censorship will lessen the difficulties of the next generation's adjustment to further impending societal swings of the pendulum. In fact, there are some signs that despite the distortions of our press reporting, sexual "possession" is no longer so dominant an answer to the need of security. The partnership approach to marriage is replacing the male dominance. This new 1976 home will shift our mores from the father dominance inside of the home. Much nonsense is written about the rule of our males by our females, and vice versa. However, the mere recognition of the problem of dominance is a step forward, although the change will come not so much from discussion as from the environmental shifts to be experienced in the next decades.

The male will no longer be symbolized as the provider for his wife while at the same time competing in the labor market with the unmarried and married female —a confusing status to say the least. The historic male role of dominance, from his days as hunter, are at an end. The machine will provide much of the male's contribution, and both parties to the home will together acquire, use and dispense. Plato, in his *Republic,* foresaw the need of women for work—work for which they qualified equally with men. The closer identification of men and women in jobs, in the homes, and most important, in the education of the children, will reduce the myth of instinctive clash and in time will seal the joint venture of home partner· ship. How soon or how far the sexual effects of such new folkway will develop is for others to guess. Segregation by sex in schools, prisons and reformatories will of course continue to give way before these new forces. No longer will men play house on their boats just because they were called "sissy" when playing house in childhood. No longer will women have to parade their concealed inferiority to the male by dressing in male attire. Oddly enough, and only for biological reasons, women should wear the pants. Above all, it seems to me that new discoveries in the area of sexual drives—Freudian and otherwise—will develop at a rate not unlike the sudden spurt of man's knowledge about fission. The piercing of the literary taboo was an essential forerunner, but with that accomplished in our courts and with the gathering of essential facts on its way, the next twenty years may show more progress toward discernment of the glory and mystery of the sexual drive than has been seen since the biblical restraints and fears first pervaded our cultures.

Cultural patterns, sexual or otherwise, ordinarily do not reflect with alacrity a change in environment. People usually are grooved into patterns, which are accepted and hugged with affection, even though their lives are quite empty of joy. The one exception that history teaches us with respect to rate of change is the rapidity of shift in very basic attitudes during war, floods, disasters, or under dire threats to freedom or survival. I don't mean to say that the changes of the new energy-leisure world will supply the exact moral equivalents of war when, to man's constant surprise, fortitude, sacrifice and fellowship become the predominant motives for behavior. And still the social revolution of the next decades will come close to evoking during peace the best in man, comparable to the best in war.

And this change without the bugle call will be an invitation to adventure. At the same time our patterns of desires will become more personal. Since leisure excitements are scarcely capable of standardization to the same degree as the proffer of goods for sale at shops, individuality will express itself more freely. Not in terms of loafing away the play hours. In fact, the exact opposite reaction will probably take effect. The hobbyist—whether carpenter, bird watcher or fisherman—rides his leisure with an addiction experienced by few working people other than the highly skilled engineer, the writer, researcher or others who enjoy creative occupations. The family of 1976 will attest to this when it is time to prepare the dinner, and father is repairing the fence, mother is weeding the garden and the children are making, doing or watching something that has become, in a real sense, part of themselves. Time means little to the man with the paint brush or the girl gathering her first collection of shells or bugs.

This drive, this expression in terms of action, carries many implications. The conversation in such a family will be less of the narrative rehearsal type which marks so many folk who live only vicariously on the work of others. We all know the noncritical empty talk that merely narrates the plot of a play, or sets forth a calendar of social events. Those who enjoy their own tests of their own skills are less desirous of telling what they did. Joy rests in doing, not telling. Moreover, they are apt to build up periods of silent thought. The problems they face in their joywork contain ponderous solutions. Moreover, such thinking soon leaves the specific for the abstract, the sequential for the causal.

But far more important, such lives can scarcely escape the joys of trial and error. Trial because it tests one's own ability, and error because it belongs to the trier and is not part of mass-produced standards of error. One's own mistakes never assume the same kind or degree of chagrin that follows from failing to meet some goal set by one's family or associates. Although these occupied individuals will create standards of their own, and although their standards will have a relation to the best examples of the work among the leaders in society, such leaders, of necessity, do not belong to the Jones family. Cults of painters, astronomers or sailors will of course exist, but with no serious effect on the prestige of separate, lone, self-satisfying neophytes. There is no par, as in golf, that must be striven for in weaving, playing the recorder, or carpentering in the home workshop. The competition is with one's self and not with the neighbors.

Such patterns, surely impressed on the young generation of 1976, will touch our most critical failure of the past years. I refer to the opposite of aggression. The fear of adventure leads to misery by default and to less than man's full potential, because of fear of losing prestige standards given to us by our associates and seldom custom-cut or homemade. No analogy to yearning for the new icebox with a great swathe of needless chrome, because the neighbors have one, will appear in the play and fun of the 1976 family. Every man will create his own prestige. And when that occurs man will take more chances. He can more readily bear a bruise to his own dream and ego than the pain he experiences by running foul of public approval.

It is hard to appraise the loss to man's potential for a full life by his present inaction. Acts of omission are just as much action as acts of commission, but they are never disapproved in the same terms because they are less easily discernible. It is not easy to attack a negative. In brief, in the new-leisure-full-breadbox world we may approach a balance between the overcompensations of aggression and the timid defaults of never taking a chance. Maybe the real answer to the insecurity of overaggressive people is the outlets provided by running risks and treating life as an adventure. Nor am I impressed by those who fear, in such an individualistic society, a serious lack of socially needed limits to what at times may be reckless adventures with life. Few have ever lived fully. Few, if they did, would not be restrained by instincts of nonhurt to others, as well as by instincts of preservation of their own ego. In any event, man will play life that way when his roof and food are assured and his income is sufficient to navigate through life with vim. That the product of such activity will not be of a supreme artistic caliber as tested by the greatest of the great is quite irrelevant, for the object of prime import is that more and more people go out after the full life. When that happens, the mathematical odds are that more good, or even supreme artists will appear out of the millions who play or sing or fiddle for their own sake, but are not necessarily imbued with the passionate self-confidence of the very great.

This type of living will affect all our folkways. Every athletic record of our day will be smashed. The records I've seen broken in the pole vault, high jump, mile and two mile will be viewed with curious amusement in 1976. Some say: "This can't go on forever. When do we reach the final world's record?" This mystic question evades the all-pervading value of effort for effort's sake. Possibly team play, subjected to regimentation and discipline, rather than the expression of free individualism, will be the forte of the efforts of the dictators. At least that is the way the scoreboard looks at the moment.

The craving for narcotics and excessive alcohol will decline as people need fewer spurs for courage, and less forgetfulness. Gambling may not decline, but when pursued it will be as a game of chance and not as a drug. Legalized it will be, for by what reason shall the state nurse-girl such frailties of man? Exposure of the owners of *organized* betting, and public disclosure of the odds will be the limits of the proper function of the state.

The Ten Commandments will be brought up to date. The five-day week has already outmoded the solitary seventh day for rest. Honor thy parents will be replaced by parents behaving so as to deserve affection. Coveting thy neighbor's chattels will, despite the last dying efforts of the advertising gentry, give way to emulation of the neighbor's valid attainments and pursuits of a self-contained way of life. The guileless will come into their own and those with physical infirmities will not be subjects of sentimental pity, an attitude that thwarts the fuller life for the less fortunate.

The adventurous spirit will explore a revision of our clumsy calendar, and the social register will evaporate. Precious jewels will revert in value to the days when, in Europe, diamonds and carbuncles were polished only for children. Even humor will change, as a secure people will not need the comfort of a joke at the expense of others.

We will be less reluctant to hide from ourselves our own deficiencies. Then and only then will we adhere valiantly to the gospel of disclosure—based on a conviction that most "sin" disappears when exposed to the light of day. Full disclosure to ourselves will grow into an ethic of full disclosure between us and our government. The only limits will be seen when disclosure interferes with our ability to confer, inquire and search for debatable or contested truths, or where intimacy demands the reserves of secrecy. In the search for accuracy we will forego the educational advantages of an informed public, through television and movies, since these media interfere with the difficult art of weighing conflicts of testimony.

People will be more like themselves, and different from the mob. By no means do I believe that virtue will always, or even mostly, dominate human behavior. In my profession I have seen too many good people hurt and even destroy other good people. I have seen the cupidity and insecurity that has led to foul and indefensible action. But seldom, except with the sick of mind, have I perceived acknowledged evil motives.

The new life, the entirely new experience of man in this new world, will create changes, good or bad, and I hold that the good will predominate and far outbalance the evil. I abhor the dogma—man is inherently evil. I decry it. Man is potentially good and tender, limited only by prior environment. The new setting will invite and make possible the best—and the best is unbelievably heartening. This change will be resisted by the insecure and the faint of heart, but it is hard to believe, against the figures and facts I have presented, that some great beneficence will fail to flow from the profound and rapid changes in the material aspects of our national economy of new opportunities.

Birth and marriage and death will be treated with the respect they deserve. The present insult of the burial rackets (the present expense is about one and one-fourth billion dollars) and the marriage show-off expenses of more than that amount, will give way to a spiritual approach to these, the outstanding events of our experience on earth. Curiosity will grow in our culture when people are not driven by the necessities of survival. Then the desire to catch and record fleeting gems of intuition will enhance our happiness and wealth. We will not require illness to gain the necessary repose and relaxation. To illness and idleness man owes many of his great discoveries: Archimedes, idle in a tub; Darwin, an invalid; Einstein, sick; Scott, crediting his best work to that precious half hour between waking and rising. The joys of discovery will come to those who are teased by the unknown, a sensation seldom experienced by the tense and busy.

Although work habits and the uses of logic and reason are essential tools for accomplishment, Bacon's hunch, in 1605, will be accepted—that we owe more to chance than to logic for the advancement of art and science. We will have time to observe things as they are, and our new renaissance will grow on the rejection of things as accepted. On such attitudes our new education will predi-

cate the scholastic recognition of the "feeling content" that
lies in intuition. As a people we will be as excited about
the "hows" of nature as the "whys."

Not all of us will possess the gift of grasping chance,
that inexplicable factor of so many of man's important advances. Not all of us will pursue the deductive approach
of Aristotle or the inductive schooling of Bacon. But
surely our leisure world will afford man his first mass environment of invitation to imagination and research. We
will avoid some of man's prior great losses that occurred
because discoveries came before man had knowledge
enough to recognize the novel. We will apperceive what is
in front of our eyes, and not only what lies behind them.
Every human, to lesser or greater degree, has the capacity
of hypothesis, imagination, comparison and reason. And
this capacity, affected by environment, can be taught. Even
the art of intuition is not exclusively a matter of genes. In
fact, for some purposes the less informed are often the best
equipped to grasp new principles. They are less thwarted
by traditional acceptance of formerly held ideas. Reason is
not the only tool for discovering the mysteries of life. Dis-
satisfaction and curiosity will not only be enhanced, but
these attributes of the explorer will be detected at early
ages by simple, accepted tests. In Pavlov's terms, we will
live in an era where all can afford the time needed for
gradualness, where unorthodoxy will not be disdained,
where humility will encourage healthy disagreement
among people of good will and where passion for the answer to our curiosity will not only encourage research but

will help to gather a harvest of answers to our questions.

When Jefferson showed his disdain for mass democracy and preached the values of the aristocracy he only foresaw, as DeTocqueville later wrote, that people in a democracy often prefer to be equals in slavery rather than unequal in freedom. But Adams, Jefferson and many of the Founding Fathers, men of intuition, were unable to envisage our new world of 1976. Surely they would enjoy it—if they were to live it with us during the coming revolution of the spirit of man.

Let no one confuse my optimism with perfection. In 1976 our way of life will be far from perfect. Not all people will use their leisure for the full life, but happily the potential of fullness in life is forever to be limitless. Pride in our nation and its world symbol will be strengthened by national confidence. Such confidence will be of a new sort, for it will be based not only on acres, wealth and possessions, but on traditions of intellectual excitement, spiritual satisfaction, creative joy and recognition of mortal infirmities conquerable by man's potentials for the full rich life.

Men and women follow only those with hope. We all seek direction markers of optimism. Our spiritual road map will carry the direction pointers: 1976—This Way—Energy, Leisure, Full Rich Life.